choosingBLUE

"That which exists best in the world . . . the color of all colors, the bluest of all blues."

PABLO PICASSO

choosingBLUE

Stephanie Hoppen

**Photography by
Andreas von Einsiedel**

Watson-Guptill Publications/New York

Senior Acquisitions Editor • Victoria Craven
Project Editor • Martha Moran
Designer • Alexandra Maldonado
Production Manager • Ellen Greene

First published in 2006 by Watson-Guptill Publications,
a division of VNU Business Media, Inc.
770 Broadway, New York, N.Y. 10003
www.wgpub.com

NOTE: Great care has been taken to faithfully reproduce the
paint chip colors in this book. Because color reproduction is
not always absolutely accurate, there may be subtle variations
between the paint chip colors reproduced here and the
actual paint chips.

Library of Congress Cataloging-in-Publication Data
Hoppen, Stephanie.
Choosing blue / Stephanie Hoppen ; photography by Andreas
von Einsiedel.
        p. cm.
Includes index.
ISBN 0-8230-0669-7
1.   Blue in interior decoration.   I. Einsiedel, Andreas. II. Title.
NK2115.5.C6H664 2006
747'.94--dc22

2005018090

Manufactured in China

First printing, 2006

1 2 3 4 5 6 7 8 9 / 14 13 12 11 10 09 08 07 06

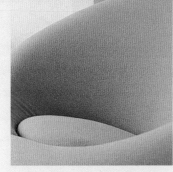

cont

PHOTOGRAPH COURTESY MAIRA KOUTSOUDAKIS

ents

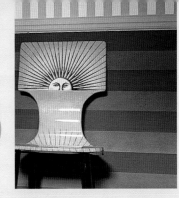

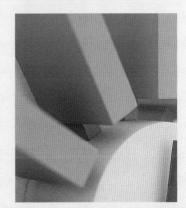

Theatrical or what? This is a dramatic sitting room with studied
touches reminiscent of a stage set. There is very little there, so
the elegant navy sofa is firmly center stage.

preface

Blue is the most common color in the world. It's the color of the sea and the sky and it surrounds us on a daily basis. But blue isn't just an accident of nature—we've invited blue into our homes because it is somehow second nature. We know that there are more blue rooms, more blue china, and more blue fabric than exist in any other color.

What I hadn't realized was that in the English language there are countless words that mean blue—and it was this diversity that became the starting point for this book. It is a vast color with an enormous range and, in my view, it has become the color of the decade. We start with sky blue and sea blue, but now think about the color of midnight and the color of dawn. Think azure, turquoise, aquamarine, indigo, teal, air-force blue, navy blue, lavender, duck-egg blue, periwinkle, cornflower blue, cobalt, lapis lazuli, sapphire, Wedgwood blue, Ming blue, powder blue, ice blue, Mediterranean blue—one can go on and on and I haven't even started on the aubergines, prunes and muddy mauves that are part of the blue family at the red end of the spectrum.

Blue was always the safe choice for the home—a comfortable and easy way to use color. After all, all the blues go well with each other and a mixture of blues is always a winner. This rule still stands, but today there is a totally new way of using the endless varieties of blue.

In the past, decorating with blue tended to mean blue and white with maybe a touch of sunflower yellow. Not any more. In the 21st century, blues are accented with acid greens and raspberry, with bitter chocolates and steely greys. Today's blues are whatever you want them to be: conventional, chic or cutting edge. Blues are news and they are exciting as well as beautiful, brand new and yet comfortingly familiar.

In this book we're going to look at blues for the 21st century and how to use them in exciting as well as soothing ways. We've got blues for every mood and season: Cape Cod blues at the beach, smart, lacquered midnight blues on the Upper East Side, chic navy and beige toiles from Paris—all in all a wonderful visual treat showing how blue is new and quite thrilling in its versatility. And on a practical level, we've researched and chosen all the vital shades of paint, together with shades that accent, tone or complement the main color.

Stephanie
Hoppen

You think pale blue, and you think the safest of colors, but it's not the case any more. Pale blue has gone all edgy and modern — replacing all those safe white walls — and I find it a fantastic look. You have to be brave. To create this new atmosphere you have to chuck out the pretty pastel patterns and all the conventions associated with baby blue and team this brave new beautiful color with the clean, chunky lines of modern architecture. Bring the color of the sky into a room and you can start looking at this color with new eyes. It's a color that goes brilliantly with all the components of the modern interior: glass, pale wood, polished plaster, shiny lacquers, metallic surfaces, and natural stone.

Blue goes urban. A slate blue called Soft Chinchilla is the perfect foil for the witty Perspex chairs, the sculptural table and the sweeping views of San Francisco.

PHOTOGRAPH BY DAVID DUNCAN LIVINGSTON, COURTESY JEAN LARETTE

new ways with pales

Mixing
the Blues

Blues inevitably go with each other and by using pale blue as a background color, you can unleash dramatic patches of indigo, teal, mauve, and intense cornflower blue. If the new pale blue is used as a secondary color, it's given a background not of white but of putty or clotted cream. But blues and creams, delightful as they certainly are, represent the safe route. I feel a real change in the air here and I'm not alone. In the hands of cutting edge decorators such as Tim Hobby and Keller Donovan, pale blue has

[OPPOSITE TOP AND BOTTOM]
This apartment was designed
by Jean Larette, a young,
Californian decorator on
House Beautiful's list of top
designers.

PHOTOGRAPHY BY DAVID DUNCAN LIVINGSTON,
COURTESY JEAN LARETTE

[LEFT ABOVE AND BELOW] An
unexpected combination of
pale blue and bitter chocolate
turns a small, featureless room
into a work of art. The strong
shapes of the day bed and table
defy further ornamentation, and
the blue gives the room a real
sense of its own personality.

picked up bold and unexpected color partnerships
from all over the spectrum. They are mixing the palest
of blues with dark, bitter chocolate browns and acid
greens, combining periwinkle blue with strong
tobacco, adding splashes of orange and egg-yolk yellow, or a frisson of silver and lavender. The result? I
don't think the blues have ever looked better.

Selecting the Color:

I find color to be the driving force behind each of my projects. My favorite colors are often in the Benjamin Moore color fan. One of the most useful aspects of selecting a Benjamin Moore color is that they offer small jars of the individual colors that I can paint onto poster boards which we can then use to narrow down our top choices. I have the client place the sample board in various areas of the room and view the color in both sunlight and evening light.

Once the color is chosen I often carry the color chip with me and use it for selecting the fabrics, wood finishes and the carpet. It is wise to be sure the color chosen coordinates with the existing artwork. If we have a very strong picture that will be used in the room, the wall color must provide the perfect backdrop.

The Paramount:

At the Paramount, a glass tower high above the San Francisco Bay, I find the use of blue to be bold, daring, and confident. I love to contrast blue with black, steel, and the reflective surfaces of the glass and chrome. It works well with the smoky grey Philippe Stark chairs. The blue feels crisp, fresh, even masculine. In this setting one can imagine taking off one's stilettos and enjoying an ice-cold martini. Blue used in a modern space should feel clean, cool, and assured.

Jean
Larette

PHOTOGRAPH BY JAMES GARRAHAN,
COURTESY JEAN LARETTE

"Growing up, I always **connected the color** blue with my father. It was his favorite color. He was cold, impersonal, and moody—I hated the color blue. Of course, maturity changes everything. I now think of blue, in its many forms, as one of the most soothing, non-boring colors. It has become the **perfect background** for some of the most interesting and beautiful interiors I have created."

JACKYE LANHAM

[PAGES 14-15] An urban bedroom. The bold and simple scheme is given a surprise touch of homely comfort in the form of donkey-brown faux-fur fabric curtains—not a choice that would automatically spring to mind, but one that works surpassingly well. Crisp white linen and smooth metallic components pick up a tinge of blue from the walls. The furniture and fittings shimmer in this calm, refreshing space.

[ABOVE] Simple shapely chic in a typical townhouse sitting room. The pale blue chimney wall and the limestone hearth are the focal point. Glass shelving in the flanking alcoves does not distract, allowing the eye to dwell on the bold lines of the rug, the luscious curves of the dirty-green chair and the strong painting. This room has a wonderfully organic feel.

[OPPOSITE RIGHT] Adobe chic. A youthful crash of washed-out colors inspired by a woven cotton dhurrie. The pale blue makes the facing wall recede, so you have the effect of a horizon beyond the orange-red ziggurat, making the room feel bigger and airier. If the wall had been simply painted white, it wouldn't be nearly as appealing.

[OPPOSITE LEFT] Glass brick walls separate kitchen from dining room, and the faint blue tinge they pick up from the kitchen beyond makes them look like a stack of cool ice cubes. Strong accent colors on the table give the scheme a real kick.

WHAT'S NEW WITH BLUE

One of the freshest ways to deal with blue is to accent your pale blue rooms with new and exciting colors such as these:

Chocolate browns look great with blues:
Benjamin Moore Forest Brown 2105-10

Benjamin Moore Maryville Brown HC-75

Try adding a bit of zing with the shocking pinks:
Benjamin Moore Peony 2079-30

Benjamin Moore Bayberry 2080-5

Here are some powerful darks:
Benjamin Moore Stunning 826, a fantastic navy

Benjamin Moore Cherry Wine 2080-30 is a gorgeously rich Burgundy red.

Creams are far "newer" than whites:
Benjamin Moore Colonial Cream OC-77

The color of blue eyes
and blue sky—a color
that appeals to everyone.

"I love pale blue. It is a color that looks
great on everyone. Every time you
think it is about to fall out of fashion,
there it is again. Clothes, furniture,
accessories and rooms always look fresh
in powder blue."

TIM HOBBY

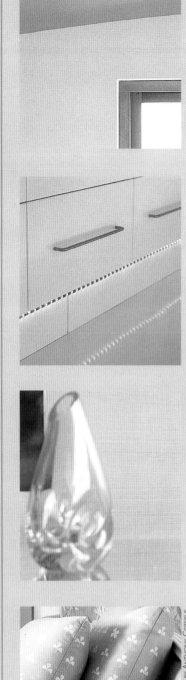

The ultimate cool box—a perfect, if totally unexpected, setting for a magnificent example of African art. The blue makes the emptiness of the space reverberate. Can you imagine, even just a couple of years ago, anyone contemplating
these minimalist surroundings and reaching for the blue paint?

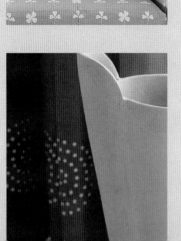

pale blues

Ice Blues

Blue is an intrinsically cool color and with the ultra-cool lustre of a pale icy blue, the effect can range from pale, frail, and pretty to cutting edge and sophisticated. It is also the color of that shimmer of blue in mother-of-pearl, and although you can't exactly cover your walls with this lustrous coating, there are some wonderful pearly accessories, from mirror frames to sensational cutlery handles, that will pick up and reinforce the quality of this elusive color.

What you want to achieve with these blues is a refreshing dose of cool, not an unfriendly ice bath. In order to achieve this, icy blues, if used as the background color, need to be carefully balanced and complemented or else deployed as subtle accents to lift other color schemes.

The Ice Blues

Paint texture can contribute as much to a room as color. Icy, shiny blues will give you a bit of a chill, while pale chalky flat finishes are warmer. Chalky shades have a receding quality that makes a room seem spacious and lively. Chalky creams look good with pale duck-egg blues. Beware of brilliant whites, they make the blues look "yesterday."

BENJAMIN MOORE ICY BLUE 2057-70

BENJAMIN MOORE CUMULUS COTTON 2063-70

BENJAMIN MOORE WHITE SATIN 2067-70

BENJAMIN MOORE WINDMILL WINGS 2067-60

BENJAMIN MOORE SUMMER SHOWER 2135-60

FRANCESCA'S PAINTS MOTHER OF PEARL

FRANCESCA'S PAINTS SALT LAKE 1

FRANCESCA'S PAINTS GALINA 1

To go with ice, the neutrals:
BENJAMIN MOORE CREAM 2159-60

FRANCESCA'S PAINTS CREAM

© JASON BELL

Blue is the color of the decade. Lately, I've been using blue in most of my projects and I find that at least 70% of my clients lean towards some range of blue when doing their homes. There is nothing more soothing than waking up to a pale blue room, seeing the shadows cast from leafy trees outside that flutter on the interior walls. The kaleidoscope of blues created from a situation like this is extraordinary.

Ice blues are the most soothing of all to me, as well as the most difficult to work with as it's easy to overpower them. I like to stay in the paler green family to accent ice blues—I like to use mints. Whites work with almost all blues; the yellow whites seem to make the icy blue appear dirty. Grass green accents in small doses incorporate a fun flair.

As a general note on blue, I think one of the most important rules to stick to when using them is the following: test, test, and test, before applying. Due to the abundant amount of blue light that we get from the skies above us, all shades of blue are going to show up differently in different rooms. The moving sun and its warm light can make one shade of blue look like different colors on each of the walls in the same room. It is best to test a blue in the actual room where it will go, as you can tell how the natural light is going to affect the color at different times of the day. Then you can observe the changes with every passing hour of light.

A pale blue room gets stronger with each wall that is coated, so test it first, then observe it. Be willing to cut the blue by mixing it 50/50 with white to achieve what you think you were going for in the beginning.

Jason
Bell

[OPPOSITE] This dining area has been kept light and airy in order not to take up visual space. The icy blue walls make a fantastic backdrop for the black-and-white photographs and the delicate iron furniture. Against white, this arrangement would seem stark and dated; against blue it is modern and sculptural.

[ABOVE] A deliciously cool bathroom gets an overall breath of blue from an irregular ceiling painted the color of a glacier with the sun shining through it. The blue reverberates around the soft white walls and the aluminium panels on bath and cupboard doors. The wooden surfaces and the chunky little window frame negate any cold, clinical aspects.

[OPPOSITE LEFT] Detail of a cool cupboard. The ice blue interior is lifted with a subtle trim of aubergine and a mirror framed with mosaic.

[OPPOSITE RIGHT] A detail of a laminate cupboard teamed with structural glass. The green glow of the glass and the blue tinge of the shadows epitomize the cool, calm feel of a glassy blue the color of an iceberg.

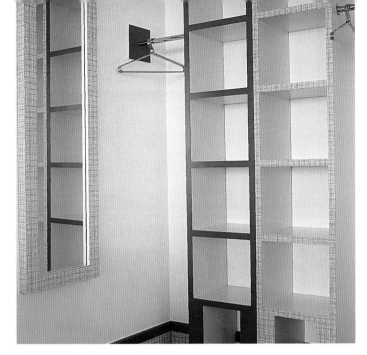

Calm Space

Ice blues should soothe rather than chill. Team them with natural wood and pale stone and they will give a room an air of calm serenity. Add a metalled surface, or an expanse of glass, and the whole room will reverberate with an energy you simply don't get in an all-white room. It's an amazing color to use with glass bricks because there's something about the thickness of structural glass that brings out the shimmer in the blue.

PHOTOGRAPH BY LAURIE LEONARD, COURTESY TIM HOBBY

I am especially fond of the color I call "Powder Blue" and I tend to be known for using it in varying ways in most of my design projects. When studying this color, I realize that there is no color that I can think of that does not look great with powder blue. I find myself pairing it with rich chocolates and woods, such as beautiful powder blue leather dining chairs with a rich Wenge wood table, or a powder blue mohair upholstered bed that sits on an ebony floor between two Chinese red lacquered nightstands.

When you think of it, greens are beautiful with this color, reds are great with this color, oranges, pinks, beiges—all look great with powder blue.

Recently, I had the opportunity to decorate my mother's home when she moved to Atlanta and I gave her several color palettes to choose from for her décor. One of those palettes included multiple shades of blues, from powder blue to a rich Wedgwood blue and multiple shades in between. This is the palette she chose and the result was incredible. A 40's French influence mixed with antiques was our foundation for creating a wonderful and beautiful home for my mom. When it came to accenting with other shades, soft pinks became the natural choice as the combination was both feminine and elegant.

In sharp contrast to my mother's home was a contemporary condominium on Ocean Drive in South Beach. The home owner requested a palette of all white: white floors, white walls, white furniture, white sheers, and even white artwork. The striking oceanfront condo was very dramatic and very stark, and yet something was missing. I added several innovative lamps that cast soft shades of colors in the room, which the home owner could control at his leisure. Additionally, I added soft blue vases and photographs of water and blue skies that added a sense of calm to the room. The result was incredible.

Personally, when I think of favorite colors that I always return to, blues are top of my list. They evoke a sense of peace and calm. They reflect other colors in beautiful ways and they pair with most any color in the rainbow. I find this color throughout my wardrobe as I think it is the one color that everyone looks great in.

Tim Hobby

Accents
for Ice

Keep to the soft end of the almost no-color spectrum if you want to balance an ice blue. You can not go wrong introducing soft whites—a limewash would look lovely—or delicate silver greys and sandy shades of beige. Harsh, shiny brilliant whites are to be avoided: they dazzle the eye and overwhelm the subtlety of the barely-there blues.

[RIGHT AND BELOW] Ice blue in a relaxed ethnic seaside setting. This ice blue is found, surprisingly, in homes in mountain villages of Morocco—a country normally associated with vibrant blues, greens and pinks. But you can see here how deliciously cool and refreshing it is. The walls are the color of the morning sky and they make the perfect backdrop for the scuffed painted floor, white limewash, old rafters and a vibrant massing of colorful cushions.

[OPPOSITE] Pale blue paint and glass are natural soul mates.

"I have found my favorite accent colors against the paler blues leans to the brown family. Darker is better for a more sophisticated look. Lighter shades of **beige/cream only** open the door and call out for yet another punch of accent, sometimes the perfect green, sometimes orange. My tendencies are now leaning towards many blue rooms outlined in brown. The **brown is** normally chosen from a fabric that I start with. It may only be a shadow in the stem of a flowered pattern that appears on a blue background print, but I make it a goal to pop that color out (always the most unexpected)."

JASON BELL

"The color orange is a beautiful color that has many lives of
its own but lends itself to walk hand in hand with blue.
Choosing the right shade is usually key, as I think coral
orange can be magic with pale blue. It can be the color of
Sunkist orange and be sportier than ever with navy blue."

JASON BELL

When an all–cool blue room needs livening up, be bold and try a dash of vibrant lemon yellow or a startling acid green. Pink is good, too, from a blush of rosy pink to a zinging fuchsia, but be wary of orangey-reds—they're aggressive colors that can suck the living daylights out of pale, bleached-out shades such as these.

[PAGES 26-27] Blue accents in this modern kitchen reflect on the ceiling and shimmer through the glass brick walls. A riot of color on and around the table: strong red, burnt orange, yellow, and cornflower blue shows how accent colors flourish in this environment.

Accents for ice:

Materials that add lustre, not color:
silver, aluminium, stainless steel, mother-of-pearl, Lucite, glass.

To add a contrast:

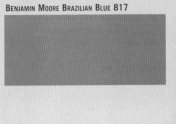

BENJAMIN MOORE BRAZILIAN BLUE 817

BENJAMIN MOORE MIDNIGHT OIL 1631

BENJAMIN MOORE BLACK

A pavilion in a country house garden that has all the feel of a seaside cabin thanks to the smart blue trim around the walls and ceiling. It's the weathered blues of the sofa cushions and the soft blue on the painted floorboards that give this room its timeless appeal.

Atlantic Blues

These are the pale blues reminiscent of northern Atlantic beaches, where the light is soft and sometimes grey. The quality of light is so essential when judging color that it's something I think people are aware of almost subliminally, which is why traditional colors work so well in their proper environments.

Atlantic seaside blues are a case in point. These are, after all, the shades of blue with the same tonal values as the northern beaches they evoke: the watery blue of the sky, the white light, the bleached yellow of the sand dunes, and the sea-washed green of the grass.

"On the Atlantic Ocean, which is a deep blue green, I choose cool, clear, crisp blues and whites. Anything that makes one feel neat, tidy, and freshly washed. The deeper, clearer blues just feel right here."

JACKYE LANHAM

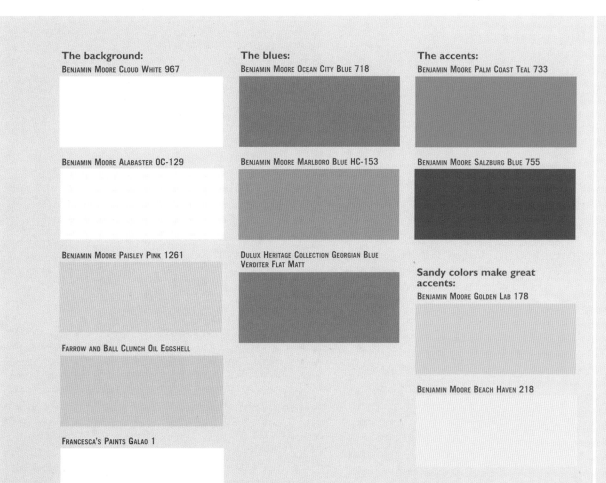

The background:
BENJAMIN MOORE CLOUD WHITE 967

BENJAMIN MOORE ALABASTER OC-129

BENJAMIN MOORE PAISLEY PINK 1261

FARROW AND BALL CLUNCH OIL EGGSHELL

FRANCESCA'S PAINTS GALAO 1

The blues:
BENJAMIN MOORE OCEAN CITY BLUE 718

BENJAMIN MOORE MARLBORO BLUE HC-153

DULUX HERITAGE COLLECTION GEORGIAN BLUE VERDITER FLAT MATT

The accents:
BENJAMIN MOORE PALM COAST TEAL 733

BENJAMIN MOORE SALZBURG BLUE 755

Sandy colors make great accents:
BENJAMIN MOORE GOLDEN LAB 178

BENJAMIN MOORE BEACH HAVEN 218

PAINT COLORS

Seascapes and Sunsets

A seaside blue traditionally calls for casual but smart cotton checks and tickings—a fresh nautical look in fact, bringing the color and character of the sea right into the home. This is a versatile blue that enjoys keeping company with sunset shades of rose pink and pale plum with perhaps an

[ABOVE] A blue warmed up with wood tones and lime-washed plaster. The faded yellow apron and the weathered yellow on the cupboard doors are the color of sand.

[RIGHT] A casual stone-flagged dining room. The soft blue weathered walls are accented with warm red and the earthy browns of the mud cloth fabric displayed above the door and cupboards.

[OPPOSITE TOP] Casual, comfortable, and very relaxed, this sitting room is the perfect spot to curl up with a good book while the Atlantic breakers crash outside. The blues here get a background the color of sand and accents of warm wood, basketwork, and a jaunty dash of rusty red. The hydrangea is the perfect floral touch for this look. The papery blue flowers are just the right shade to add character to a pale scheme.

[OPPOSITE BOTTOM] A medley of checks. The traditional soft blues are spiced up in this kitchen with primary red. It's a cheerful combination—perfect for a simple holiday cottage.

accent of turquoise, reminiscent of seas in warmer climates. These soft, washed-out colors look wonderful not only as paints on the wall, but as a furnishing fabric on sofas and chairs, or as tablecloths, beach towels, and throws, and they mingle wonderfully with off-white linens.

Natural Warmth

The Atlantic Blues need warmth. Pale wooden floors add a honey-colored tone, which is good, as are natural fiber mattings of sea grass or jute. My particular favorite accent colors with the washed out blues are strong doses of indigo and denim, perhaps in the form of china or casual throws. Terracotta is another option, either as floor tiles or as an accent color. Antique terracotta pots have a wonderful weather-beaten quality about them that makes them a perfect foil with beach house blue. And, of course, with their lovely bulky shapes, they hold their own as focal points in both traditional and modern settings.

The backgrounds:
BENJAMIN MOORE MONTEREY WHITE HC-27

BENJAMIN MOORE DOVE WING 960

The blues:
BENJAMIN MOORE PICTURE PERFECT 743

BENJAMIN MOORE IN YOUR EYES 715

BENJAMIN MOORE FANTASY BLUE 716

BENJAMIN MOORE WEDGWOOD GRAY HC-146

BENJAMIN MOORE COVINGTON BLUE HC-138

The accents: Look for "dirty" colors, anything too pristine would look wrong.
BENJAMIN MOORE CAPE HATTERAS SAND AC-34

RESTORATION HARDWARE SYCAMORE GREEN

RESTORATION HARDWARE BUTTER

RESTORATION HARDWARE LATTE

[OPPOSITE TOP] Here blue is used as the accent color in a surprising and effective way. The spacious and solid bathroom gets in touch with its surroundings thanks to the sea blue window frame and shutters. Other splashes of color here are subtle—a rose pink cushion and two turquoise water glasses.

[OPPOSITE BOTTOM] Bold blue stripes and a blind made from blue and white ticking are all it takes to give this seaside bathroom a soft wash of the blues.

Gustavian

This is a lovely pale grey-blue, mixed from blue, white, and raw umber and it is synonymous with the Classical Scandinavian interior and those elegant pieces of painted furniture that look like 18th century French furniture, but are somehow more user-friendly. It is a color that works brilliantly in the very white light you get in that part of the Northern hemisphere and, handled well, I think it looks really smart. It gives spaces that same enlarging and light-enhancing effect of the all-white interior without the glaring white-out that would result from stark white light on stark white walls.

"I love Gustavian grey blue—it is, conversely, a warm blue that has to be mixed each time it is used as every room reacts differently depending on whether it has many windows or few, or faces south or north. I love cream curtains with it—always cream not white. For accent, a burnt orange is my color of preference."

LARS BOLANDER

[ABOVE AND RIGHT] Very Gustavian, this room, decorated by Sasha Waddell, has grey-white walls with a very subtle blue accent. The fretwork on the furniture is picked out with an ethereal washed-out blue.

INTERIOR AND FURNITURE DESIGNED BY SASHA WADDELL, PHOTOGRAPH BY GAVIN KINGCOME, COURTESY SASHA WADDELL

[LEFT] This dining kitchen is decorated with a calming mix of blues, nothing to jar the eye. The sideboard is painted in a shade of Baltic blue that Sasha Waddell has specially mixed for her and the chairs, by Skansen, are upholstered in a simple check. The simple Swedish runner on the floor is in yet another shade of blue. On the dresser is a mix of vintage enamelware, again all in different shades of this fabulous color, proving that all shades of blue work well together.

INTERIOR AND FURNITURE DESIGNED BY SASHA WADDELL, PHOTOGRAPH BY GAVIN KINGCOME, COURTESY SASHA WADDELL

Many styles of interiors, furniture, and colors are named after Prince Gustav, who in the eighteenth century visited the court of Louis XVI. He was very influenced by the French court and when he returned to Sweden as King Gustav III, he introduced this French style to his royal palace.

This pale blue/grey is achieved by mixing a clear blue with white to get the chalky quality and then a touch of raw umber to knock the color back. The more raw umber used, the greyer the blue becomes, so it needs a delicate touch.

In this bedroom with the canopy, I have painted the walls in the palest of blue grey with a hint of a motif in the palest of pink so it is hardly there.

The floors are bleached floorboards and I have painted the furniture the same blue grey so it has an ethereal quality. The fabric is a Swedish print in a dark blue on an off-white background and the bedcover in an off-white, nothing to jar the eye so this room is calm and restful, perfect for a bedroom.

Sasha Waddell

[LEFT] A lovely room of grand proportions that uses this gentle blue in a self-striped wall covering. It is the perfect complement to the gorgeous Aubusson carpet and upholstered chairs that have faded to a delightful lived-in degree. The accent colors here are faded pinks and the glowing gilt of serious picture frames.

"You only realize that this is blue when you look at it against grey or green—it is such a faded, subtle color and is perfect for use with Swedish furniture and interiors. It is subtle and faded and fine."

MONA PERLHAGEN, CHELSEA TEXTILES

This soft Gustavian wall color gives the dining room a tranquil elegant atmosphere. It is important to note that this color changes tone with the amount of light found in the room at any one time.

On the Walls

The Classic Swedish interior would have this subtle color on all walls and woodwork, with furniture of pale or painted wood, pale floors, off-white upholstery and a delightfully grand touch of over-the-top such as a massive chandelier dripping with crystal droplets. The classic accent piece is an upholstered chair in a fabric with a cream ground and a strong blue pattern. It is worth remembering that the traditional Swedish textile vocabulary includes toiles and florals as well as the ubiquitous checks and stripes.

Handling a Complex Color

Gustavian blue is a difficult color to handle well. Because of the grey element in it, you have to be very careful it does not end up looking cold. I would team it with a soft white, never brilliant white, and if the ceilings of the room are low, I'd paint the ceiling in an even paler shade to lift it a little. Pink is the recommended accent color to warm the scheme up. If you want subtlety, go for a pale pink. If it's vibrancy you want, go for fuchsia.

[PAGE 37] It is a spare look, more fined-down than the French or English equivalents of Classic style. In this restrained bedroom the elegant lines of the Empire style furniture are beautifully set off with a pale satin blue and gilt accents, underpinned with a rich dark blue carpet.

Soft Blue

A soft and gentle blue that is pale but still strong, looks wonderful in both modern and traditional settings. It is a true color that sings out irresistibly, like a pair of bright blue eyes.

A soft pale blue sounds a bit fey, but it absolutely isn't. It is a color that can be all things to all men and women. Furnish your soft blue room with dark wood, sisal matting, and bold artworks with strong contrast colors. Add a bit of tobacco and chocolate and you've got a distinct masculine edge. If you want feminine and pretty, choose soft white as the neutral color and add in pale woods and interesting pastel accents.

A fresh look at tradition: A soft periwinkle blue gives this hallway the look of a Wedgwood vase. The blue needlework rug acts as a wonderful underpinning and the mellow antique furniture and balustrades are set off to perfection.

Contemporary paintwork in a lovely traditional bedroom. The room is outlined in a stripe of periwinkle blue with the walls in a softer shade. The lack of fussy decoration focuses the eye on the gorgeous beds. Again it shows the power of a pale blue background to showcase beautiful pieces of furniture.

The Traditional Palette

This gorgeous blue is a perfect foil for lovely faded antique fabrics and rugs, for busy interiors full of delectable collectibles, for bedrooms furnished with lace and mahogany. It is a well-behaved and well-brought-up color that goes with everything and yet does not lack personality.

[ABOVE] This is a room designed to show off a collection of Brunschwig fabrics. There are five different patterns in this room, all in a similar tone, and the effect is soft and gentle, creating a room where nothing shouts at you and there are no accent colors to distract from the garden views.

PHOTOGRAPH BY ANTHONY COTSIFUS, COURTESY BRUNSCHWIG + FILS

[RIGHT] A day bed upholstered in a pale blue-grey fabric set against a grey-blue slate floor. The chair is upholstered in a cool broad stripe and the screens are covered with a silver metallic wallpaper that really bounces light around the room. A very calm space—an invitingly cool retreat on a hot day.

PHOTOGRAPH BY ANTHONY COTSIFUS, COURTESY BRUNSCHWIG + FILS

[LEFT] A traditional, elegant, and comfortable London drawing room with elaborate curtain swags in a darker shade of the blue on the walls. The palest color is used on the largest expanse, and darker shades pull in the edges. It s a lovely calming feeling.

[BELOW] I love the simplicity of this room with its beautiful blue bench and cushions neatly placed between two cupboard doors. It is a simple, subtle and very effective use of a touch of blue.

The backgrounds: Soft blues look good with soft, clean background colors:

FRANCESCA'S PAINTS SAND 1

FARROW & BALL CLUNCH OIL EGGSHELL

RESTORATION HARDWARE THE RIGHT WHITE

The blues:

BENJAMIN MOORE WINTER LAKE 2129-50

BENJAMIN MOORE SUMMER BLUE 2067-50

BENJAMIN MOORE WINDMILL WINGS 2067-60

FRANCESCA'S PAINTS ROYAL BLUE

[RIGHT] Here is the exception that proves the rule. It is one of the few occasions I'd recommend using white with blue; normally I prefer cream or beige for today's look, but in this very traditional bedroom, white is the correct solution. There's something about white bed linen that can't be beaten. The massive mahogany wardrobe doors look like a setting for *The Lion, the Witch and the Wardrobe*.

[BELOW RIGHT] Traditional Biedermeier furniture in glowing fruitwood is upholstered in crisp blue and white stripes. A collection of cups on a lovely mahogany table point up the blue. This is a great example of tradition with attitude.

[BELOW LEFT] A lovely perspective painting, predominately blue, is accented with ethnic hand-carved wooden toys and decoy ducks.

[OPPOSITE] The exposed brickwork and beams speak of French country houses. The blue here is an accent color to shades of stone and wood. On the floor is an antique Agra dhurrie. There are blue cushions on the sofa and the chair, and dominating the whole room is a huge painting with a blue background. It's a warm, mellow room.

"Isn't it interesting how this shade of blue works so well with every kind of wood, from the dark glow of mahogany and fruitwood to the pale honey of stripped pine?"

STEPHANIE HOPPEN

In the Modern Context

Soft blue can have a startle factor. Imagine it used all over the walls and accented with red or orange, dark brown or lime green. For a more subtle approach, you could upholster just one piece in blue—a curvy sofa or a modern chair for instance—and let the color sing out from a sea of pale wood and white walls.

[RIGHT] A fresh approach to soft blues. A perfect example of how, in the modern context, blue is softened up with creams, beiges, and oyster pinks.

[OPPOSITE] This room is all about shape. The squashy blue sofa is a strong presence in this traditional period room. The Perspex coffee table adds a modern touch, and the red accents contribute a necessary warmth.

PAINT COLORS

Wood—pale or dark—looks particularly good with a soft blue, as does stone from honey colors to cool limestone.

Crushed raspberry is a great foil in a traditional interior:
BENJAMIN MOORE MARDI GRAS 1342

BENJAMIN MOORE MINSTREL HEART 1297

ROSE DAMASK 2 FROM FRANCESCA'S PAINTS

A dark denim blue looks modern:
FARROW & BALL ESTATE EMULSION STONE BLUE

Saffron yellows are warming:
BENJAMIN MOORE BRYANT GOLD HC-7

LEMON CHIFFON FROM DULUX

"Living in the south brings an acceptance of the heat. Cool colors help create calming visuals. Blues, laced with green or lilac, are the most appealing and flattering in all venues."

JACKYE LANHAM

We have been asked, repeatedly, to use a particular color of blue—which for these purposes we will call Nordic blue. It is not Gustavian blue, which is much more grey, and paler. The color I refer to can be found in Scalamandre's bold check called *Brompton Plaid #30118-014*. According to the industry bible, the Pantone charts, the color is a mixture of five colors, including black.

Finding soft, non-synthetic fabrics to coordinate with "My Blue" has been a challenge. Luckily Beauvais makes a contemporary plaid carpet with several similar tones. It is called *Wilmington*, color: blue and camel. The London firm, Claremont, makes a beautiful silk damask, their *Fleurie, Bleu/Bert*, and a small silk plaid called *Faille Correaux Bleu*. But no other company in America makes any usable colored fabric, and the only paint company that makes a similar color is Kaufman, known for their organic, brown-based paints.

I do not totally understand why my clients fall passionately in love with this color, but they do. It is soft, easy to live with, and perhaps just complex enough not to be boring.

Stephanie Stokes

[OPPOSITE] A soft blue bedspread gives this masculine leather-clad bedroom a gentle touch.

[ABOVE] Casual and relaxed, this room feels like home with its washed out indigo fireplace, stripped wooden floors and curvy blue armchair. The Damien Hirst–type spots on the wall bring the room bang up-to-date.

[RIGHT] A sculptural vase that demands attention. Soft blue is an unusual color for a modern porcelain glaze and it looks wonderful against red.

Satin
Ribbon Blue

The same blue with a lustrous surface redefines the color yet again. It creates the classic, sultry boudoir look of precious silks and glossy satins shimmering in candlelight, but with a fresh, modern angle. It is the perfect look for a bed-

[OPPOSITE] The ultimate modern blue bedroom with a padded satin bed that adds luster and comfort to a monochrome scheme.

[RIGHT] Urban bedrooms are getting smaller with the constraints of space and the desire for huge living areas. This bedroom with potentially claustrophobic dimensions has been turned into a clam blue jewel box.

[BELOW] The one accent of color in this bedroom is a red flower in a blue vase placed on a space-saving shelf. The orangey-red is a brilliant foil for a soft blue.

room, where the sheen and glow from the iridescent surfaces soften and warm the intrinsically cool tones of blue. But you don't need to confine shiny satins to the boudoir—you could upholster a day bed in satin blue to add a sensuous touch to the living room, and pile it with silken cushions in smoldering purple or enigmatic indigo.

To take the sheen to the walls, use silk taffeta curtains and a glossy blue paint. But a shiny blue ceiling could be a step too far—paint ceilings in paler shades, or even a soft shade of white.

There's nothing like a blue that has been battered about a bit, one that has aged well and faded so it resembles something organic, like a bird's egg or a pebble rather than a man-made skim of acrylic paint.

The Seychelles resort is called North Island and it is 100% environmentally friendly with a calm, Zen-like atmosphere. The sun beds are of unbleached calico. Subtle touches of color come from the silver grey decking and the sea foam blue of the towels.

weathered blues

Inspiration from the Landscape

There is no better way to understand the look of weathered blue than to indulge in a visit to a Seychelles resort designed by the renowned architects Silvio Rech and Lesley Carstens. Their vision is evident throughout this marvelous resort, and their inventive use of organic materials draws the natural landscape into even the smallest interior and exterior architectural details.

[ABOVE] The seashore inspired the sand, the sea-splashed blues and the silvery greys that form the color palate of this subtle scheme.

PHOTOGRAPH COURTESY MAIRA KOUTSOUDAKIS

[LEFT] A natural feast for the eye. A beaker of recycled glass and a tic-tac-toe game made of driftwood and terracotta.

PHOTOGRAPH COURTESY MAIRA KOUTSOUDAKIS

[OPPOSITE TOP] Attention to detail. Food is served on platters of iridescent turquoise that look as organic as the food in question with its appetizing accents of lime and coral.

PHOTOGRAPH COURTESY MAIRA KOUTSOUDAKIS

[OPPOSITE BOTTOM] One of her more inspired touches was to sew coral beads onto the corners of the sofa cushions. The coral is a wonderful, natural accent color for a sea-washed scheme.

PHOTOGRAPH COURTESY MAIRA KOUTSOUDAKIS

"Chalky colors give wonderful texture to the walls and this keeps changing with the light."

FRANCESCA WEZELL

Rech and Carstens brought in the talented South African designer Maira Koutsoudakis to decorate and accessorize. Maira took her inspiration not from the bright, lively blues of the Indian Ocean but from the colors of the landscape: the worn gris taupe of the granite, the pale teal blue of the vegetation. And she chose mottled, textured, faded finishes so the resort feels as if it has evolved organically, over time, from the surrounding rocks and sand.

new ways with pales

53

The source of Maira's inspiration for the washed-out turquoise color came from this door on a wooden shack.

Maira has used her colors in proportion to their strength on a downward scale. The main color is a sandy off-white called papyrus, and she's cleverly chosen a matt and mottled finish for maximum light play. Floors fall in the same area of the spectrum, and she's used a gorgeous pale limestone for those. Shades of green-blue ranging from soft grey teal to sea-green turquoise are used sparingly as the main color accent, and she's added tiny flecks of coral to enliven and amuse the eye.

The result is that the colors have a soul: the pale teals and shingle greens do not look man-made. She's banished all hints of the slick and the new by rubbing back the paint colors and washing all the dyed fabrics and then washing them again and again. The charming hints of sparkle and color come from little bracts of recycled, crushed glass African trading beads that look as if they've been battered by the ocean for decades.

These lovely faded colors and textures are, in one sense, unexpected, but they convey no sense of shock—they are familiar in that they are the age-old colors of nature—but they've been used in a new and interesting way to create a gentle, energizing environment. The whole project exudes harmony and there's not a harsh note in it.

"Pale smoky teal is one of my favorite colors and I blend this with the warm grey-taupe colors of wood and granite that reflect the ever changing vistas of the sea. Good contrast colors to smoky teal are coral and sand."

MAIRA KOUTSOUDAKIS

The neutrals: You need weathered looking neutrals too. Here are some lime washes and soft, chalky colors:

FRANCESCA'S PAINTS SALT LAKE 1

CROWN PAINTS MOONLIGHT

BENJAMIN MOORE BREATH OF FRESH AIR #806

RALPH LAUREN CABANA BLUE GLAZE

Color

The interiors of North Island explore the tonal nuances of color and non-color, elusive, evocative, emotive blues—subtle sage, greige, duck-egg blue, stone, chalk, coral, sand, turquoise, aqua—the blues are celebrated in all their mottled, hand-dyed, overdyed, bleached, faded, shiny, matt and coarse character.

PHOTOGRAPH COURTESY MAIRA KOUTSOUDAKIS

The color of the atolls seen from the air, all turquoise, white and sand, informed a very large part of the visual language of the interiors. Nature's manner of manipulating materials, stripping color down to a fainter, calmer version of the original, suggested the use of only natural materials which age well with the sun, humidity and sea spray. The immediacy with the elements becomes a factor in the ever changing appearance of furnishings and fixtures, where, for example, the natural blue dyes overlaying each other suggest to the annual visitor the slow, subtle passage of time.

Creating a contrast to urban life (that often may be complex and clinical), the island interiors create a tranquil retreat that brings us in touch with fundamental pleasures—the solidity of stone, the grain of wood, the scent of sisal, the brush of silk. Texture and color are all-important—the rich, glowing hues of burnished brass and solid wood, the warm tones of rough-hewn sandstone and unbleached linen. Natural materials are comforting to the touch and have a timelessness—they wear well and the patina of age and seaside life only add to their sensual appeal.

Color has personality; from sharp, piquant turquoise to serene, softly seductive duck-egg blue, the distinctive personality of each color is individual and intuitive and informs the overall mood.

Though blue has traditionally been associated with tranquility and coolness, our use of the spectrum of blues—and the way nature has a hand in the transmutation of these colors—has yielded surprising secrets. Blues can have the dark, somber severity of indigo or the bright, inquisitive impishness of turquoise, even the mature sophistication of faded blue-greige. The blues have age, personality, and attitude, the critical thing is to identify the one that suits the brief.

Maira Koutsoudakis

The New Neutrals

First it was magnolia, then it was taupe, now you can have a neutral color that is a real color—and it's blue. There are fantastic ranges of exciting fabrics and paints available now, featuring the palest washed-out blues from the almost turquoise to pinky lavenders. These new neutrals give a whole different dimension to a scheme because, like the old neutrals, they go with every color under the sun, but unlike them, they've got loads of personality, they're lively, and they zing with possibilities.

Old and New Ways with Color

New technologies give us fabrics that react to light, that shimmer and shine in ways we could only dream of. But when you get to the paint, it's the old technologies that are making a comeback. Thick, creamy limewashes with wonderful textures, and handmade paints with natural pigments point up the subtleties of pale colors and give them life.

[ABOVE] A brilliant accent color is used here in a weathered finish, so the little drawers have been given texture but haven't lost their vibrant tone. The burnt coral on the walls is an inspired choice.

[ABOVE] An antique effect has been created with a powder blue and plenty of gilt.

[OPPOSITE PAGE] Bernie de la Cuona is producing some of the loveliest neutral fabrics around. Just take a look at these and then tell me you'll be opting for the plain white linen!

Blues so washed out they can be used as neutrals

The accents:

Natural colors: Any natural color, like sand or limestone, works well.

BENJAMIN MOORE OLD STRAW HAT 337

BENJAMIN MOORE CAPE HATTERAS SAND AC-34

Bright corals: It is hard to find a flat paint color that replicates the three dimensional impact of real coral. It's a texture story.

BENJAMIN MOORE STARBURST ORANGE 2010-30

BENJAMIN MOORE SANGRIA 2006-20

RALPH LAUREN PLATEAU WITH POPPY GLAZE

FRANCESCA'S PAINTS ROSE

Bright turquoise: Imagine this accent as a piece of bright blue glass washed by the sea.
For flat paint colors:

BENJAMIN MOORE CARIBBEAN BLUE WATER 2055-30

BENJAMIN MOORE BAHAMAN SEA BLUE 2055-40

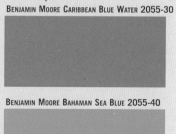

P A I N T   C O L O R S

Blues toward the green
end of the blue spectrum
are colors associated with
plants, landscape, and wildlife. They
are wonderfully easy to live with, and if
used boldly, they make a strong contemporary statement.

Teal at its most elegant, making a wonderful backdrop for the exquisite
Biedermeier sofa, the gilt-framed portrait, the glowing wood shelving, and the
well-ordered leatherbound volumes that give the room the warmth it needs. It's
a real Georgian English country house color.

green blues

Teal

Here is a delightful shade of green-blue with a name borrowed from a small duck. The duck itself comes in a blue-winged or a green-winged variety, and the distinctive color of its plumage enables it to blend in with the woods and water that create its natural habitat. It's a strong, subtle color that I absolutely adore, particularly as an accent color in the home. Not surprisingly, it works wonderfully on painted outdoor furniture too. Being neither grass green nor cornflower blue, it blends effortlessly whether indoors or outdoors.

A Strong Tradition

Pale teal colors are almost grey, reminiscent of water running over stones, and they make good wall colors as long as there are plenty of warm shades around. I think that vast expanses of unrelieved teal would make a room feel gloomy and waterlogged.

The stronger the teal color, the more distinctive it becomes. Although it looks deliciously modern, teal as a paint color has a long heritage. It's a Shaker color, used on furniture more often than on walls, and it features in many examples of hand-painted folk art from decoy ducks to antique wooden signs. But you'd be wrong to associate the color with the historical and the folksy. It also turns up as a fantastic modern glass pigment and a stunning ceramic glaze.

Traditionally, stronger teal colors are used as accents,

as all but the softer shades would be overwhelming as an all-over solution. For living rooms, think of striking silk lampshades, bold porcelain vases, teal colored glass with the sun shining through it, and a large oil painting with a teal blue background. It's the perfect color for the front door of a red brick house, and imagine how a run of deep blue-green hand-glazed back-splash tiles would liven up an all-white bathroom or kitchen.

"Teal blues can be mystical when mixed with fiery red-oranges; this combination can be used in so many directions, from whimsical to sophisticated."

JASON BELL

[OPPOSITE] The decoy birds are a dark teal, the tin table is that nearly-black Parisian green, and the fresh checks and stripes have been chosen in a turquoise blue. Set against a weathered grey garden bench, these could be nature's own.

[LEFT] A seaside retreat has window frames painted to match the old kitchen table that has been pressed into service as a desk. The pink peonies are a lovely color accent, picking up from the faded pattern on the chair cushion. Again there's a great mix of blues here; there is indigo in the carpet and a pale ice blue on the bookcase against the far wall.

Teal works well with glowing woods and stone as well as flashes of dark pink and mulberry.

Blue teal:
BENJAMIN MOORE MOZART BLUE 1665

FRANCESCA'S PAINTS ICE HOUSE BLUE

BENJAMIN MOORE AEGEAN TEAL 2136-40

Green teal:
BENJAMIN MOORE NEWBURG GREEN HC-158

THAT COULD BE MELLOWED BY MIXING IT WITH
BENJAMIN MOORE KNOXVILLE GRAY HC-160

A brilliant peony pink:
BENJAMIN MOORE SECRET RENDEZVOUS 1341

A gunmetal grey:
FRANCESCA'S PAINTS BLACK OLIVE

For mulberry:
BENJAMIN MOORE NEW LONDON BURGUNDY HC-61

Always remember you can bring the color down a bit. Aubergines and purples in the same tonal range work well too:
DULUX RUSSIAN VELVET.

BENJAMIN MOORE SEDUCTION 1399

BENJAMIN MOORE FIRE AND ICE 1392

Friends of Teal

Teal sits at the point of the spectrum where blue meets green. Traditionalists use it with brick reds and whites. A bolder hand, however, would mix it with colors of equal intensity, such as mulberry, burgundy and gunmetal grey.

[LEFT] A perfect color for shutters, blending with natural stone, climbing plants and the natural pigments of limewash.

[ABOVE TOP] A lovely toile in shades of teal and cream adds a wonderfully mellow element to this room. Toiles in sharper colors give out an altogether different message.

[ABOVE BOTTOM] The teal lampshade is perfect zing of color in this traditional warm English sitting room with its mellow autumnal colors.

[LEFT] Teal tiles against a soft grey white have an essence of modernity and a warmth that white bathrooms do not often have.

[BELOW] With teal in your white kitchen, it's impossible for it to look stark and uninviting. The color is the passport between shiny white laminate and the warm wooden work surfaces.

Some random thoughts on blue:

I have a theory that people view colors differently due to the pigmentation in their eyes. Mine are hazel, green with yellow flecks, that change with the clothing I am wearing. I find I am drawn to colors that hint of green—yellows, greys, blacks, and always blues—pale, deep, musty, faded, dragged, cracked, glazed, bright or dusty, but always with a touch, a direction, an overture, of green (teal, aquamarine, mallard, robin's egg and sea glass).

Blues are great neutrals to yellows, pale mint, lavender, and brown, as well as flax, hemp and linen. Black, whites, and creams create interesting combinations with blue, particularly when used in textures and objects. Some examples would be ebony furniture, Estruscan pottery, Delft ware, blue and white transfer ware and lots of textured white and cream fabrics.

Blue can be tricky in dark, murky areas as they have a tendency to "grey" if natural light is dull. Coastal areas are natural places for blues as the light reflections are perfect—the sun is clear and they feel cool.

Jackye
Lanham

Turquoise

The blue that hovers on the edge of being green was the national color of Ancient Persia (now Iran), the source of the oldest and finest turquoise gemstones. Ancient Persians trusted in this lively color to ward off the evil eye. Their buildings sparkled with this fortunate color thanks to a turquoise glaze, derived from copper and used to decorate bricks and tiles, often in conjunction with an intense blue derived from cobalt oxide.

Cool, Clear Water

Another strong association with turquoise is the shimmer of the sea as the result of the sun shining from an intensely blue sky on shallow water and white sand. Of course, it's a color that immediately evokes exotic locations. You may think that distinctive shimmer is a sensation only sun and sea can create, but once you've seen iridescent polyurethane used as upholstery, you'll realize how much things have changed.

[ABOVE] An inviting sea that runs the gamut from translucency to deep dark blue. In the foreground is a touch of turquoise blue glass.

[LEFT] A pretty shabby-chic kitchen. By taking turquoise down to the palest end of the spectrum, the color can work in a traditional setting, enhancing stronger colors.

[ABOVE TOP] A wonderfully strong 18th century Chinese color that looks amazing with touches of gold. It is a bold Georgian color that makes a stunning backdrop for elegant 18th century furniture.

Turquoise for Every Mood

Turquoise has a high profile, so it tends to be used as an accent color, in vases, painted furniture, tiles, and fabrics, and it certainly brings a joyous touch wherever it goes (in fact the Ancient Persian name for the turquoise gem was *pirusheh,* meaning joy). Backed with white, turquoise is casual at the seaside; tricked out with gold it could grace the walls of a palace; and teamed with wild fuschia or acid green it changes character again.

Faded turquoises are easy colors to live with, and I think they look wonderful all rubbed back and faded on the walls of a seaside cottage. Weathered turquoise appears traditionally on Provençal shutters, and looks particularly atmospheric against yellow ochre walls. Faded turquoise can also look pretty spectacular in an urban setting, particularly in a room used mainly by night where it does not have to fight with a dull grey daylight. Imagine it, teamed with hints of garnet red, in the grandest of dining rooms.

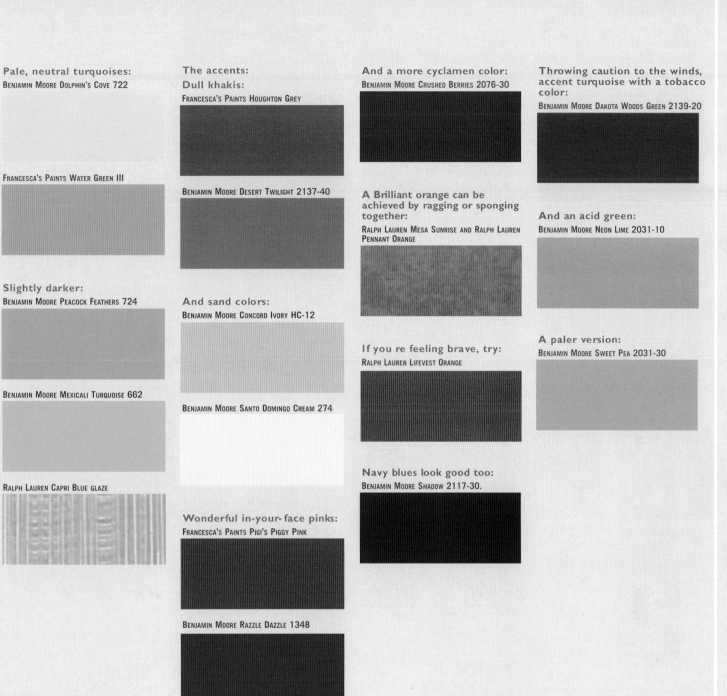

Pale, neutral turquoises:
BENJAMIN MOORE DOLPHIN'S COVE 722

FRANCESCA'S PAINTS WATER GREEN III

Slightly darker:
BENJAMIN MOORE PEACOCK FEATHERS 724

BENJAMIN MOORE MEXICALI TURQUOISE 662

RALPH LAUREN CAPRI BLUE GLAZE

The accents:
Dull khakis:
FRANCESCA'S PAINTS HOUGHTON GREY

BENJAMIN MOORE DESERT TWILIGHT 2137-40

And sand colors:
BENJAMIN MOORE CONCORD IVORY HC-12

BENJAMIN MOORE SANTO DOMINGO CREAM 274

Wonderful in-your-face pinks:
FRANCESCA'S PAINTS PIGI'S PIGGY PINK

BENJAMIN MOORE RAZZLE DAZZLE 1348

And a more cyclamen color:
BENJAMIN MOORE CRUSHED BERRIES 2076-30

A Brilliant orange can be achieved by ragging or sponging together:
RALPH LAUREN MESA SUNRISE AND RALPH LAUREN PENNANT ORANGE

If you're feeling brave, try:
RALPH LAUREN LIFEVEST ORANGE

Navy blues look good too:
BENJAMIN MOORE SHADOW 2117-30.

Throwing caution to the winds, accent turquoise with a tobacco color:
BENJAMIN MOORE DAKOTA WOODS GREEN 2139-20

And an acid green:
BENJAMIN MOORE NEON LIME 2031-10

A paler version:
BENJAMIN MOORE SWEET PEA 2031-30

[OPPOSITE TOP] In my search for the ultimate turquoise statement, I finally found it in my bedroom at the Birkenhead Hotel, at Hermanus, perched on the rocks outside Cape Town. The huge chair dominates the entire room, and yet is in complete sympathy with its surroundings. Background colors are teals and creams and a wonderful ginger shade of floor tile.

PHOTOGRAPH BY JAN HOBERMAN, COURTESY STEPHANIE HOPPEN

[OPPOSITE BOTTOM LEFT] Typical Provencal wine bottles resting under an orange tree. Turquoise and orange are wonderful sunshine colors.

[OPPOSITE BOTTOM RIGHT] A lovely seaside kitchen with toned-down shades of turquoise illustrates how a good weathered base color sets you free to be bold. Here a mix of different elements, from African mud cloths to bright red in the shelf alcove, are effortlessly pulled together with accents.

The French Country house look is timeless, comfortable, relaxed, beautiful, and gloriously faded round the edges.

It speaks of rooms that have grown up alongside generations of the same family, effortlessly blending old and new with charm and grace. It is a style concept that has captured imaginations all over the world and it is constantly being interpreted and re-interpreted, studied and copied. It has survived and actually grown stronger as a look with the advent of minimalism, and I suspect it will always be the dream of about 90 percent of all householders. Why? Because it represents a truly beautiful, relaxed lifestyle that is actually achievable.

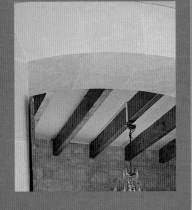

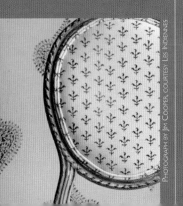

The epitome of the French Country look with weathered shutters, a sand color on the walls, and a wrought iron table set for lunch on a shady terrace. It's a totally uncontrived look.

french country

The Lifestyle

It is impossible to conceive of the French Country style without the color blue. It includes a huge range of differing blues, all of which are equally at home in this Provençal fantasy world, wherever it is situated, from California in the west to Istanbul in the east, from Sweden in the north to Cape Town in the south.

The blues associated with Provence range from the near turquoise you see mottled and faded on sun-blistered shutters, to deep indigos hand blocked onto linens, and cornflower blues faded like old tapestries. Most of the Provençal blues are in the true blue spectrum, but I also love to use the pales and soft blues as a retreat from the hot sun, the cool, weathered Gustavian blues and, of course, lavender—the very scent of the area.

Generally, French Country blues are used, not as an overall background, but as a secondary color. In the sitting rooms you see touches of blue in glass and china, in lovely patterned wallpapers, checked and striped cottons, and in the graceful designs of toiles and cruel-work curtains.

[ABOVE] Tremendously weathered painted furniture in a stunning shade of hydrangea blue that works well with faded gilding and an old gilt escutcheon plate.

Eating areas are of prime importance, preferably spilling out onto a patio with weathered terracotta pots, painted metal furniture, and shades of Marcel Pagnol. There will always be blue somewhere, in the plates, glasses, or tablecloth or in checked cushions casually thrown on the chairs.

And what could be more relaxing and romantic than the French Country bedroom, with drifts of white muslin tied to elegant iron bedsteads with blue bows, gorgeous, shapely armoires filled with freshly ironed linens embroidered with initials, beds covered in cotton throws or French quilts with the tiniest of discreet blue and white patterns?

[OPPOSITE BOTTOM] A high-ceilinged village house in Menton has softly lime-washed walls and a wonderful painted armoire in a distressed shade of grey blue that works well with the stone and the terracotta tiles. Cushions on the sofa pick up the color.

[ABOVE] The rough stone walls and ceiling of this beautiful vaulted dining room are warmed with a glowing wooden table and accented with curtains in periwinkle blue. The curtains are lined with a patterned fabric that gives them a certain swagger.

[LEFT] As blue and white carpets go on old stone floors, these naturally dyed Agra dhurries are the perfect answer. The color fades as it ages. All of the blues in this room tone in together—patterns, stripes, everything.

[ABOVE LEFT] A totally different take on the French Country theme—it's a more modern look—mixing two or three clean blues ranging from turquoise to peacock, teamed with soft whites.

[BELOW LEFT] A pretty bedroom under the eaves exudes a cool calm. Blue and white bed linen is teamed with camel-colored throws and a camel and blue rug on the floor.

© GINNY MAGHER

Blue in Provence

Blue is my favorite color. I use various shades of it in most of my projects. And I have used it generously in both my Atlanta home and my home in Provence. Blue is an obvious color choice for decorating in Provence. It is a color that is part of the vernacular of this region. Every tourist who visits Provence talks of the "French blue" color they want for their homes. But if you know this region well, as I do, you know that there are many shades of blue that constitute French blue: the rich, intense blues in a Van Gogh painting, the crisp blue of the Provençal sky on a clear day, the sun faded shades of blue on house shutters in small villages dotting the countryside, and the indigo blue of the old Provençal printed fabrics favored for tablecloths here. These are just a few of my inspirations for the blue colors I chose to use in my decorating scheme in our Provençal home.

Our master bedroom is enveloped in a lovely indigo blue-and-white toile, my kitchen has lavender blue walls and a cornflower blue and white tile backsplash. My everyday Gien china is blue and white and the fabulous 18th century Chantilly plates that hang on the wall in our entrance hall are blue and white as well. I have soft blue heart linens on our beds and more blue and white delft tiles in some of the bathrooms. I use blue-and-white check tablecloths outside, white linen tablecloths with a birds egg blue monogram and scalloped edging from Edith Mezard for the inside, and lush blue throw pillows on the chaises at the pool. I crave the big blue Provençal hydrangeas as centerpieces for our alfresco summer dining and I can't do without my woven blue market baskets for Wednesday morning market day in St. Remy. We even have a blue car we keep here. I could go on and on about all the wonderful blue in Provence. As you can see, I really do love blue and to me there is no better color in all of its shades to use in Provence.

[ABOVE]   A traditional French Country bedroom with a brilliant blue lining to the half-tester and a strong blue carpet. The walls are a lovely warm shade of ochre limewash.

Ginny Magher

> "French blue is the most requested color my clients ask me to use in their decorating schemes."
>
> GINNY MAGHER

[ABOVE] Blue in a supporting role. The stove and a painted rush-seated chair are chosen to complement the blue tinge in the bricks. The big success story in this room is the touch of screaming orange on a cupboard door.

Supporting Colors and Textures

This most desirable of looks relies on a mellow background of wood tones, natural stone, weathered terracotta, and sunny ochre yellows. Traditionally, golden sunflowers have been considered the perfect foil for blues in Southern France. They grow all over the area and are the symbol of summer with their turning heads and brilliant hues. It seems to me, however, that in the 21st century I am seeing much more imagination and individuality in the interpretation of this style. Good modern accent colors that I've seen working well are greens and pinks and daffodil yellows.

[LEFT] Wooden chairs and a massive hutch are painted in a softly distressed shade of the softest blue. The limewashed walls are the same color as the sunflowers, the signature blooms of Provence.

[BELOW LEFT] Clean but still unmistakably French Country, using a Delft blue teamed with bone colored furniture with slight accents of distressed gilt. The bone color is in fact the background shade of white typical of Delft china.

[BELOW RIGHT] Faded terracotta is a color synonymous with the French Country look. This delightfully cluttered dresser pulls all the accent colors together, from ochres and tomato reds to deep blues and cream. The collection of china plates, all of them with a different design, have these colors in common.

French Country Colors

Neutrals for this look should be soft, limewashed and chalky. If you can't source a genuine lime-wash, try:

RALPH LAUREN ICELANDIC POPPY

BENJAMIN MOORE DECORATOR'S WHITE.

The basic blues need to be faded and weathered. Some soft blues are:

FRANCESCA'S PAINTS SALT LAKE I, II AND III

Stronger blues for accents:
BENJAMIN MOORE BLUE DRAGON 810

GEORGIAN BLUE VERDITER FLAT MATT FROM THE HERITAGE COLLECTION AT DULUX

BENJAMIN MOORE SAPPHIRE ICE 808

BENJAMIN MOORE BLUE LACE 1625

BENJAMIN MOORE WEDGWOOD GRAY HC-146

BENJAMIN MOORE WINTER LAKE 2129-50

RALPH LAUREN SUNBLEACHED BLUE GLAZE

BENJAMIN MOORE AQUA MARINA 816

RALPH LAUREN CATAMARAN BLUE GLAZE

DULUX NIAGARA BLUES

The accents:
Shades of terracotta:
BENJAMIN MOORE ROSETTA 038

FRANCESCA'S PAINTS DUNE 45 II

BENJAMIN MOORE SAVANNAH CLAY 047

For a deep blue:
BENJAMIN MOORE DOWNPOUR BLUE 2063-20

A dash of tomato red:
RALPH LAUREN LIFEVEST ORANGE

Ochre colors and sunny yellows are a must:
BENJAMIN MOORE AUGUST MORNING 2156-40

BENJAMIN MOORE SUNFLOWER FIELDS 174

FRANCESCA'S PAINTS SUN YELLOW FROM THE EARTH COLLECTION

FRANCESCA'S PAINTS LOUISE'S ORANGE.

[OPPOSITE TOP RIGHT AND BELOW RIGHT] The fabrics look so good because they are handprinted. Les Indiennes use real indigo, and the same printing techniques as was used in the 18th century. It's really not "perfect," which is what makes it so great, and the colors fade elegantly with age.

[TOP RIGHT] PHOTOGRAPH BY JIM COOPER, COURTESY LES INDIENNES
[BELOW RIGHT] PHOTOGRAPH BY TRIA GIOVAN, COURTESY TRIA GIOVAN

[OPPOSITE BOTTOM LEFT] Pretending to be French Country on an urban rooftop terrace. A mixture of blue and white fabrics on mattresses and cushions is relaxing and very chic. The generous blue dishes add splashes of color and the sun shines softly on lime-washed walls.

Then and Now

French Country was always associated with the mellow tones of fruit wood furniture, checks and stripes, toiles, and block prints all jostling together in a heavenly panoply of blues. But recently I have noted a strong movement towards stripped and whitened furniture that looks even better with soft and true blues.

Here are patterns for people who don't like patterns, but how they have changed! Not so long ago, checks were windowpane, tartan, or gingham, stripes were uniform and if they were blue they were true blue and white. The new ranges of checked and striped fabrics I've seen recently are in a whole new area. They use blues in completely unexpected ways and mix and match scales so the eye is constantly surprised. And there's another revolution in the choice of fabrics. I've seen utilitarian ticking stripes woven into sumptuous silks, and wonderful grey-blue flannel pinstripes that have walked out of the tailors and into the furnishing store. Anything goes!

A dramatic masculine use of blue, with the curtains looking like patchwork rather than a check, and geometric shapes in a gunmetal grey.

checks and stripes

© F. SCHUMACHER & CO.

[RIGHT] Another example of how well cream goes with blue. It was always blue and white before, but now it is definitely cream. And there's a wonderful mix of patterns from the toile on the chair, the checks in the curtains, and the nubby stripes of the throw.

[BELOW RIGHT] A really new take on blue with a two-tone slate color on the bottom part of the wall and paler horizontal stripes above. The stripes on the curtain include a bizarre mixture of aubergine, orange, black, and pale pink. It's like a Navajo rug on speed.

[OPPOSITE] Shades of Venice with navy and cream stripes in a bedroom that is neither too masculine nor too feminine.

New Stripes

Missoni is doing bold stripes in luxurious silks that don't betray a hint of uniformity—they are mixing shades of blue, sandy yellows, greens, and plums to amazing effect. Ralph Lauren continues to innovate with a striped fabric collection that includes bright new blues mixed with black, grey, and cream. Many retailers offer wonderful rug designs—asymmetrical blocks of stripes in blues, greys, creams, and reds that tease the eye. Ticking has shed its predictable origins and come out in a flurry of gorgeous sandy yellows and pale blues.

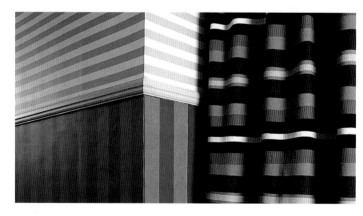

The new stripes are clever and interesting with all kinds of subtleties woven in: look for stripes that have the thinnest possible borders in complementary tones that just fuzz the definition of what a stripe actually is.

"I find checked and striped fabrics look wonderful as linings for elaborately embroidered curtain fabrics. It's unexpected, and it looks really smart from the outside."

MONA PERLHAGEN, CHELSEA TEXTILES

Check out the Checks

Some of the prettiest checks are subtle and faded, teaming blues with creams and yellows. Chelsea Textiles and Kravet have brought out ranges of checks that defy definition: there are so many to choose from, and in so many colors, more often than not with blue as the dominant color.

[RIGHT] A tucked-away corner that has been turned into a sleep-over room. Gingham curtains can be pulled to give privacy. The bright blue sofa bed is a solid statement as are the broad stripes on the window blind. A very low-key, functional scheme accented with shades of natural cane and sisal.

[BELOW] Smart loungers take a crisp blue check. A practical alternative to the ubiquitous white linen.

[OPPOSITE TOP] An interesting mix held together with checks. The comfy daybed is upholstered in a blue-and-white check with striped pillows. The engravings in their black and silver frames are mounted on a deep blue board. Lamps are made from blue and white vases. Accent colors come from the Welsh blanket throw and the red Chinese trunks. Curtains are edged with the fabric used on the cushions.

[OPPOSITE BOTTOM] A really bold mix of checks and stripes that play havoc with perceived perspectives. Flouting every rule in the design book, this bold scheme is dominated by two inspired one-off chairs.

"Some of the newer stripes and checks are interesting in that they incorporate oranges, reds, ochres, and greens, all adding a new dimension, reminiscent of those fabulous antique Scandinavian mattress tickings."

MONA PERLHAGEN, CHELSEA TEXTILES

Modern and Traditional Approaches

Checks and stripes have always worked well together to produce an orderly riot of non-pattern pattern that's both fresh and interesting, and also supremely easy to live with. They are so versatile that they can be used in both modern and traditional interiors, either as full-on curtains, wallpapers, and furnishing fabrics or in the walk-on role of cushions and blinds. And if you want just a hint, deploy checked and striped plates, glasses, and vases, to give your room a touch of striped or checkered wit.

[OPPOSITE] A very traditional crisp and clean bedroom. The stripe on the wall has a hint of crushed pink and the same pink has been used in the mounts for the pictures over the bed. Touches of pink make a blue room a little warmer.

[ABOVE RIGHT] Soft cream curtain with an overcheck of pale blue and a solid blue under-curtain. The tie is of rope and varnished wood. Very ship-shape. The blues are all different strengths of the same tone.

[MIDDLE RIGHT] An interesting way with checks. Uneven lines on a textured fabric.

[BELOW RIGHT] From a fabric collection by Schumacher—a themed collection of checks, stripes and leaves with a lovely coral spotty material. A delightful combination.

© F. SCHUMACHER & CO.

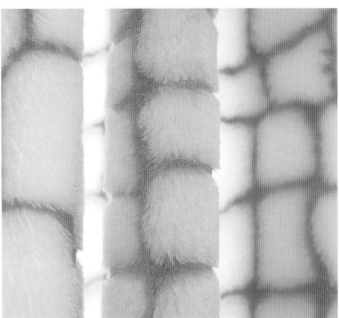

At the center of the
spectrum, pure blues
are lightened with
white, or darkened with
black until the blue
reaches the resonating
intensity of indigo.

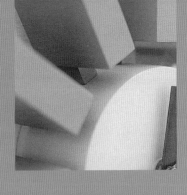

true blues

An enchanting country kitchen features a strong true blue, not with cream
this time but with thick white lace curtains. The chairs have a terracotta
stripe on the seat pads, proving that terracotta is the perfect foil for blue.

"Blue and white seems to strike a chord in many people. It has a freshness and simplicity which recalls childhood days of seaside holidays, and washing blowing in the wind. It is both calming and cheerful."

WENDY JONES, MAJOLICA WORKS

Cornflower Blue

The classic combination of cornflower blue and soft white works well in cool, northern light. It is a look that is now injected with an interesting modern twist. Bold designers are exploiting the true blue qualities and no longer confining this joyous, youthful shade to little bursts of accent color—it's going all over the walls.

The joy of cornflower blue is in its intensity. Of course it works brilliantly with every other shade of blue there is, and because of that it makes a tremendously exciting backdrop for the traditional blues of Chinese porcelain and the ubiquitous willow patterns and ginger jars, breathing new life into the old troupers. Imagine a display of traditional china against a background of cornflower blue—you've got an instant art installation.

[OPPOSITE] A wonderful cupboard with bold blue doors is filled with white china while the top shelf glows with yellow.

[ABOVE] A dressing table with attitude. Simple chunky furniture looks sculptural when boldly painted. And the border on the wall keeps the eye moving.

[LEFT] A brilliant custom-made wall-mounted clock with chunky cornflower blue markers and a touch of red in the second hand. It's a great way to use color, with the impact of a work of art.

"I love a blue the color of a Bachelor's button flower—it's a strong, clear, happy color without being too dark. It is wonderful on walls in a semi-gloss finish so that the light bounces off it."

LIBBY CAMERON

Accentuate the Positive

Because this blue is clear and true, it will flourish alongside colors quite close by on the color spectrum, such as muddy mauves and dirty greens, which would give any room a modern mean and moody look. For flashes of excitement choose bright pinks, clear reds, and acidic limes and lemons. The best neutral color is, as always, white. The true blues are perhaps the only ones that can take a totally cool white without loosing their impact, but I still think that the creamy whites look best.

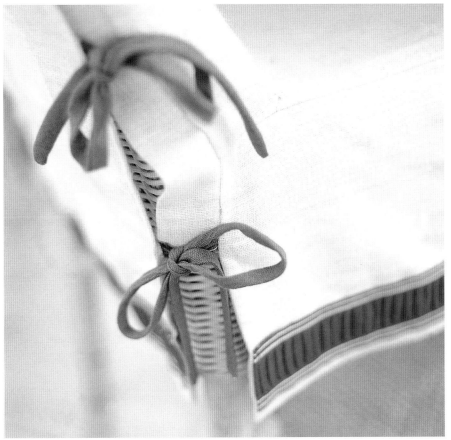

[OPPOSITE] A heavenly bedroom with every shade of blue and every shape of cushion and pillow you could possibly want, plus a lovely bedside touch of pink.

[ABOVE] An unexpected touch of blue in the form of a carved newel post on a driftwood staircase.

[BELOW] A simple toweling chair cover with chic blue ribbon detail. I think a towel-covered chair is an absolute must for any bathroom—it adds a touch of total luxury.

[ABOVE] A traditional over-stuffed chair looks really modern upholstered in this strong blue. It's a real modern, young color when contrasted with cream, and the red anemones are an inspired touch.

[OPPOSITE LEFT] Two chunky blue sofas in different materials and yet more shades of blue in the cushions. This is a vibrant, modern room with its zinging touches of orange and yellow.

[OPPOSITE RIGHT] The ducks have a view to a window with a brilliant blue step and a vivid orange door. A delicious color combination.

Blues, Neutrals, and Accent Colors

The neutrals here should be soft creams, like:

RALPH LAUREN ICELANDIC POPPY

RALPH LAUREN EDWARDIAN LINEN

FRANCESCA'S PAINTS SAND 1

FRANCESCA'S PAINTS BOILED EGG 1

BENJAMIN MOORE YOU ARE MY SUNSHINE 302

BENJAMIN MOORE CANDLELIT DINNER 295

BENJAMIN MOORE LINEN WHITE 912

BENJAMIN MOORE NAVAHO WHITE 947

Some shades of Cornflower are:
RALPH LAUREN BELLFLOWER BLUE

BENJAMIN MOORE SUMMER BLUE 2067-50

BENJAMIN MOORE BLUE LAPIS 2067-40

A really dark midnight:
BENJAMIN MOORE DOWNPOUR BLUE 2063-20

There's a lovely orange:
BENJAMIN MOORE ADOBE ORANGE 2171-30

A zingy pink:
RALPH LAUREN'S MORNING PINK GLAZE

Tomato red is a color that works really well with all shades of blue:
BENJAMIN MOORE FIRE DANCE 2171-20

Traditional Blue

Although this book is about new blues, moody blues and funky blues, I think it would be criminal not to devote time and space to celebrate the stunningly beautiful traditional blues. This is the dependable combination of blue and white on Chinese porcelain, on Delft tiles, and willow pattern. We can all picture this color in our mind's eye without even blinking. Old-fashioned blue with white is possibly the most popular combination in interior design—because it works. It is foolproof and it always looks clean and crisp and magical.

[ABOVE] Delphiniums are such traditional English flowers, and there's nothing more fabulous than an exuberant burst of blues. They give a real emphasis to a blue room and lend a pallid room a real boost.

[RIGHT] A lovely dining room with different blue and white patterns: a check wallpaper and a floral chintz on the chairs. One of the reasons blue is so popular is that all shades of blues go together. Here the blue flowers on the table pull the room together.

[OPPOSITE TOP] The oxblood red is a very traditional Georgian color for rooms that are used mainly in the evening, like dining rooms. The deep red background gives the blue accents a sophisticated feel.

[OPPOSITE BOTTOM] Very traditional French urban chic with blue used delicately throughout and a wonderful blue tapestry on the wall. A very sophisticated look that proves the theory that less is more.

"I love the new China blues from Tricia Guild's new collection—they are the classic china blue but with a **soft white** that seems to work well with the **cool northern** light of Europe and the Northern USA. Her fabrics are full of large overblown cornflowers and work **wonders with** denim-covered armchairs, chalky wallpaper, and aqua stripes."

STEPHANIE HOPPEN

Traditional Props

Elegant 18th-century drawing rooms were show-cases for exotic objects that reflected the owners' wealth and good taste. Hence the popularity of rare and precious Chinese porcelain in the form of plates, bowls and ginger jars which were tradition-ally displayed on small purpose-built shelves rather than artfully arranged in groups. In more humble surroundings, displays of willow pattern china or Wedgwood Jasperware would have to suffice, or maybe white linen with blue embroidered mono-grams, but the accent was still on the blue—a true classic blue—the one your mother told you never to mix with green.

[OPPOSITE TOP LEFT] Traditional blue-and-white china pieces mixed and matched to good effect. They look lovely set on gleaming mahogany against a soft white wall. It's elegant, wonderful, and you can't fault it. These are all originals but it is possible to get really convincing copies.

[OPPOSITE BOTTOM LEFT] Squat Chinese porcelain jars on a sunny windowsill set off with dried hydrangea heads. The shapes and the colors complement one another perfectly.

[OPPOSITE TOP RIGHT] I've always collected dark blue Bristol glass because I love the wow factor that it adds to any table. Here I've used Bristol glass candlesticks, dark blue pleated napkins I bought in California, and some bright blue bowls from my collection. *Stephanie Hoppen*

[OPPOSITE BOTTOM RIGHT] The blue china balls are the sort of thing you can buy in any good decorating shop. They add a traditional accent, like the jars and vases, but have a more youthful feel.

[ABOVE RIGHT] Blue-and-white jars combined with sunny yellows make a cheerful display for a kitchen. Just catching sight of it lifts your spirits.

[RIGHT] Nothing is more satisfying than having a complete collection of Chinese porcelain in a beautiful display cabinet. There are plates, slop bowls (originally used for tea but you can use them for soup), tea caddies, and any number of bowls. And you can see by the way they are stacked up in the cupboard that this is not a static collection, these items are in daily use.

[RIGHT] In Manchester, England, a brilliant pottery studio called Majolica Works is bringing a level of design, elegance and artistry to ceramics that compares with anything that came from ancient China. Majolica is a type of porous pottery, glazed with bright metallic oxides originally imported into Italy via Majorca. This type of pottery was produced extensively in Italy during the Renaissance.

PHOTOGRAPH BY JOEL CHESTER FILDES, COURTESY MAJOLICA WORKS

[OPPOSITE LEFT] A really modern take on a blue and white kitchen. Everything is visible; the cupboards are either open or glass-fronted, revealing a visual feast of blue and white patterns from the tiled surfaces to the dishcloths and the pretty shelf edging. It's incredibly practical, too, because you can get at everything.

[OPPOSITE RIGHT] Colefax and Fowler are one of the oldest established interior design companies and they stand for the epitome of traditional elegance. Here they have used antique Chinese porcelain plates on a table set with crisp white damask and Georgian silver. A real traditional treat.

"Instant tradition for an overbright, newly decorated room: create the illusion of sun-faded surfaces by adding lighter tints to paintwork and using a pale wash over wallpapers. For that rich antique feel, do the same using darker tints."

STEPHANIE HOPPEN

Good whites are:

BENJAMIN MOORE ROYAL SILK 939

BENJAMIN MOORE LINEN WHITE 912

FRANCESCA'S PAINTS GALAO 1

The Blues themselves:

BENJAMIN MOORE DOWNPOUR BLUE 2063-20

BENJAMIN MOORE WINTER LAKE 2129-50

BENJAMIN MOORE BLUE HYDRANGEA 2062-60

BENJAMIN MOORE GLASS SLIPPER 1632

FRANCESCA'S PAINTS GEORGIO'S WISTERIA

Accent colors:

BENJAMIN MOORE CONFEDERATE RED 2080-20

BENJAMIN MOORE CURRANT RED 1323

And the yellows:

BENJAMIN MOORE SQUISH SQUASH 311

DULUX LEMON CHIFFON

BENJAMIN MOORE LEMON 2021-20

Sunflowers on the Table

You can lift the old-fashioned blue and white combo out of the predictable and into the realms of high fashion by adding an exciting contrast color to the mix. No flower sets off a truly old-fashioned blue and white table setting as much as a jug of sunflowers. The loud, vibrant yellow flowers add a youthful dimension to the most traditional of tables and contribute a certain chic to old or odd collections of blue and white flea-market finds with plates in myriad shades of blue.

Color Accents

A burst of sunflower yellow fabric, a yellow painting or a collection of cushions will add zip and warmth to the traditional blue and white interior. Pale jadeite glass is another imaginative touch that Nina Campbell uses to such good effect. Today, decorators are teaming traditional blue with "dangerous" orange and turquoise, mixing up the blues with each other and using stronger blues as solid secondary colors rather than polite accents. It is time to be bold with old fashioned blue.

[ABOVE] A restrained display of porcelain vases and floral sprigs. Lovely tones of blue and creamy white used with an eye for shape and proportion.

[LEFT] A large hallway with a traditional hall table holding a blue-and-white bowl planted with five phalaenopsis orchids—absolutely the flower of the moment. It looks wonderful.

[OPPOSITE TOP RIGHT] The classic accent for a traditional blue is a generous bunch of sunflowers. Here they are in a hallway in a Chinese porcelain vase, adding instant sunshine.

Chintzes

Traditional chintzes are becoming more graphic and less fussy, but as with all things traditional, the classics will survive because of their timeless qualities—it's just the way we now use them that makes them relevant. Chintz on chintz on chintz looks very dated because too much busy pattern is an assault to modern sensitivities. A little bit of chintz mixed with bold patterns and strong color contrasts is pretty, fresh, and appealing.

Toile

Fabrics reinvented. A toile de Jouy is the traditional decorator's standby. It's pretty and fresh, looks good as curtain fabric, and is impeccably comme il faut. But there has been a quiet revolution against those 18th century idealized rural scenes of shepherdesses and hunting dogs. The fabric house of Schumacher, for instance, has introduced a toile depicting American wagon trains with the pattern blocked in a deep indigo.

[TOP LEFT] The lovely blue and white floral chintz fabric is used to elegant effect on this dining chair.

[LEFT] A toile-like effect is perfect for use on walls. This delightful blue and white fabric is based on "Indienne", a circa 18th-century French fabric found on an early French quilt. Patterns like these are marvellous interspersed with stripes and checks and indigo dyes to make an all blue room.

PHOTOGRAPH BY NAT REA, ©CHELSEA TEXTILES

[RIGHT] The classic interior: Classic decorators will approach a scheme from the starting point of a fabric—here it is the upholstery of the chair in the foreground. The neutral cream in the pattern has been chosen for the walls and curtains and the darkest shade for accent color—the two blue chairs flanking the fireplace. The lovely rug picks up the blue and adds shades of red. It's a soothing, timeless look, easy to live with and without a jarring note.

I n the beautiful Johannesburg home of celebrated psychologist and TV and radio personality, Dorie Weil, I noticed a very, very beautiful blue bedroom and asked her what had made her choose this very traditional coloring. *Stephanie Hoppen*

It was more a natural evolution than a choice. Because of the pace, passion, and perpetual stress of my career, I found the choice of blue and cream a natural progression. A "without sunglasses" blue was chosen for its calming effect, creating a haven which I call my "deep breath" space, a place to rest and renew and become calm again. The different blues work together and mingle in an effortless way encompassing one with a sense of peace and tranquility. The colors of the sky and the sea have always been credited with celestial peace and here one feels this.

Dorianne
Cara
Weil

[OPPOSITE BOTTOM] Traditional Provençal fabrics that can be used for bedding, tablecloths, curtains and cushions. It's a distinctive look that mixes and matches patterns and is very easy to live with.

[ABOVE AND BELOW] Two traditional bedrooms using the same hues of blue but to vastly different effect. The top bedroom is feminine and pretty with its draped four-poster and frilly valance, the other more graphic, more masculine.

Mediterranean Blues

Hot climate blues have a history as exotic and sun-baked as the sun-bleached shores they evoke. Deep ultramarine blues have their origins in a semi-precious gemstone, lapis lazuli, first used as a pigment in 6th-century Afghanistan. This intense color resonates from the pages of 14th- and 15th-century illuminated manuscripts and Renaissance paintings. It was a paint color made from ground-up gems mixed with wax and oil, and it was so expensive, more precious even than gold, that it was used sparingly and reverently for touches of splendor—such as the Madonna's robes—in works of high art.

It's an intense blue without a hint of red or green—a necessary component in a balanced palette—and it's hard to believe it didn't exist as a viable synthetic pigment until the 1830s. Since then, of course, it's become a color much associated with painters. You've only got to think of the startling blue of Matisse's *Jazz Dancers*, the vibrant signature color of the artist Yves Klein, now known as International Klein Blue and Bleu Majorelle, used famously and to brilliant effect in a Marrakesh garden by the artist and architect Louis Majorelle in the 1920s.

[ABOVE] Moroccan ceramics are a great starting point and reference for the Mediterranean look. The intense blues sit happily with oranges, reds and greens, and patterns of all kinds.

[BELOW] A stunning blue on an eccentric mosaic urn with orange accents and black beards. It's a magnificent piece, strong enough to use as a starting point for a decorative scheme.

[OPPOSITE] The Artist's blue: Boston-born Georges Sheridan, whose entire artistic life was influenced by the painter Matisse, lives and works in the Mediterranean village of Deia on the island of Majorca. The blue of his paintings is the true Mediterranean cobalt blue with almost every other color bleached out. His subject here is an odalisque, reclining on a patterned cushion, just like Matisse's muses used to do.

Georges Sheridan has always used intense color in his painting—and he has a predilection for blue. At one stage he had a Blue Period and painted many, many fine oils in a deep, azure, Mediterranean blue. Sheridan continues to always include blue paintings in each collection—he says that he finds blue a very spiritual color.

PHOTOGRAPH BY RAY FOX, COURTESY STEPHANIE HOPPEN GALLERY

Hot Cool Blues

The quintessential Mediterranean look is an intense ultramarine teamed with white. It's a color I always associate with lazy days, rough-plastered white walls, and a cobalt blue sea. It's the contrast with white that makes the blue seem bluer and the mood more a Greek island holiday than a contemporary urban loft. To keep the hot climate look going, team ultramarine with compatible strong earthy colors that thrive in bright light. You will get the look using hints of burnt-orange ochre, or the a hot pink of South American woven fabrics and that slightly dusty copper-green turquoise of Middle Eastern pottery glazes.

"Blue can be a very happy color as well as a serious one. Used with corally pinks and greens it becomes livelier and seems clearer."

LIBBY CAMERON

[ABOVE] Dark blue medicine bottles teamed with shells on a marble washstand. In the background, the indigo border and the white tiles create the perfect backdrop.

[LEFT] The ultimate hot cool blue with a Mediterranean flavor is a slice of mozzarella on a brilliant blue plate.

[OPPOSITE] Moroccan arches on the windows are picked out with blue glazed tiles. It's just a touch of blue, emphasizing the shape of the arches. Sometimes its not just the color, but the way you use it.

Ultramarine Accents

A strong blue is a dominant cool color and its effect on other colors depends entirely on context. A strong blue accent in a white room adds a frisson of chill. Set against honey-colored stone or wood, a blue will heighten the warmth of natural materials while providing respite for the eye. In a room full of strong warm colors, ultramarine comes into its own, providing a welcome counterpoint in the satisfying completion of the color spectrum.

[BELOW] A simple ethnic style kitchen that scores with brilliant splashes of blue on the tiles and yellow on the cross beam, giving the room a casual, southern feeling and evoking the sultry feeling of constant sunshine.

[OPPOSITE, LEFT TOP AND BOTTOM] These are the epitome of cool hot blues. A very modern, urban take on ultramarine. The top bathroom hums with color reflected in a mirror wall. In the room below, the strong color is broken up by the lines of the tiles.

[OPPOSITE TOP RIGHT] An old stone sink in a southern French home, the tile backsplash is very decorative with its sunny circles flanked by borders of beautiful blue.

[OPPOSITE BOTTOM RIGHT] Patterned ultramarine tiles are where, in decorative terms, the Southern Mediterranean meets North Africa. In the Americas it evokes the feel of Mexico. Here a simple copper bowl is inset into a free-form washstand.

Navy, Indigo and Denim

Derived originally from the plant Indigofera tinctoira, this deep, dark blue (now synthesized and more colorfast) was always destined to fade in the sun. It is the original Navy blue of sailors' uniforms—uniforms that faded with long service, leading new recruits to scrub away at their jackets until they looked suitably seasoned with age and experience.

[ABOVE LEFT] There's something about navy and stripes: it just exudes smartness and it's a brilliant look that can be as modern or traditional as you like.

[ABOVE RIGHT] Ultra-chic navy lacquer is a perfect foil for a golden scroll and a golden Buddha. Dark blues and shiny metallics go well together.

[BELOW RIGHT] Bold stripes make a graphic statement in an attic bedroom with a sloping ceiling. The deep blue throw and the blue-black cushions are smart and luxurious.

"Ink blue rooms are dark and **sophisticated**. The color is best used in larger rooms. I find the stronger blue rooms always seem to close the room up. Using this rich **color helps** make vast rooms feel a little more manageable. **Accents** of old gilded frames and **natural colors** like tones of creams and beige help to calm ink blue down. Emerald greens work really well in this type of room; they shine all day long and **fit perfectly**."

JASON BELL

PHOTOGRAPH BY JAN BALDWIN FOR NINA CAMPBELL'S *DECORATING SECRETS* © CICO BOOKS

Nina Campbell was the first non-American chosen to do the Kipps Bay Show House, in 2005. *Stephanie Hoppen*

Navy is a glamorous background for crystal, silver and mirrors—it is therefore a perfect color to use in a dining room—particularly one that is used principally at night. In the dining room illustrated, we see how superbly effective this is.

In the early 20th century, very dark blue dinner jackets were worn by elegant Englishmen as this midnight blue color is "profounder" than black. I think the profoundness of the color works well as an interior design color as well.

In two of my homes, the dining rooms are principally dark midnight blue and they work as day dining rooms as well as night dining rooms as the color is relieved in one case by bookshelves and in the other by a very large window.

Often, using midnight blue or a similar tone in an already dark room makes that room look purposefully dark and luxurious. A navy hall can be fun, as all the rooms that lead off it "pop" in contrast to the deep navy hue.

Using midnight blue, or in fact any really dark shade, is also a clever way to disguise an awkwardly shaped room.

Nina Campbell

True Indigo

Indigo is a living color that in its original dark state is a shade of blue that is almost darkness made visible. It is a great color, that in spite of its long traditions feels exciting and new, both for fabrics and paint. It is being used, not just for reinvented traditional designs such as tribal Ikats from Indochina and Suzani textiles from Uzbekistan, but to give a new depth and dimension to traditional Western fabrics such as paisleys and toiles. A deep indigo fabric will retain its color only if a top-of-the-range, expensively treated dye has been used, so to retain the velvety blue-blackness, keep indigo away from direct sunlight.

[ABOVE LEFT] An inviting traditional kitchen making the most of a chic alliance between deep navy, ochre and red.

[ABOVE RIGHT] Navy is a color that has come back in style with a vengeance. It's an exciting and glamorous shade of blue and an unusual but stunning choice for a bathroom as it looks so good with white and it has a wonderful sheen.

[OPPOSITE] This stunning bedspread is in a deep-dyed indigo fabric embroidered with white. It is teamed up with curtains in a floral design, with blue and white stripes and complemented with a stool upholstered in a reverse fabric, white with indigo embroidery. Indigo will fade and run with washing, and while this is desirable in a pair of blue jeans, it is a case of "dry clean only" with furnishing fabrics.

© CHELSEA TEXTILES

"Indigo is a natural color used in the 18th century, but it is as relevant and exciting today as it was then. I find indigo or midnight blue to be one of the most amazing of the new 21st-century blues. It is wonderfully dramatic and glamorous and is great with so many accent colors—silver, glass, shocking pink, etc."

MONA PERLHAGEN, CHELSEA TEXTILES

In with Indigo

Indigo looks modern with paler blues and whites, dramatic with black, and positively zinging with turquoise. You can warm it up with reds, oranges, and yellows and make it mellow with natural wood. Where I find it most effective, I suppose because it is the most surprising place to find it, is in indigo glazes and pigments on china and glass. Such a collection would look wonderful piled onto a shelf or a tabletop with a bouquet of creamy white roses.

Indigo is a great accent color for almost any look. It can be as cheerfully traditional as you like, for example on a check kitchen tablecloth, but introduce true indigo to a sheeny metallic and it's almost saturnine.

"Indigo is the color of the Indian sky at night."

SASHA WADDELL

[LEFT] Stephen Falcke has somehow managed to reinvent the concept of the all-blue, pattern-on-pattern room. It is such a far cry from the origins of this look that it can't be pigeonholed by style—it's simply an inspired way of using textures and patterns to create a wonderfully atmospheric room of total beauty. I could say a great deal about this room, but really all you have to do is look at it and see the art of interior decoration at its finest.
PHOTOGRAPH COURTESY STEPHEN FALCKE

[ABOVE] A bit of role reversal here, with the floor this time painted a shiny navy blue, crisp white walls, and a simple rag rug. It looks stunning.

[OPPOSITE] Indigo chic gives this dining room a new and very 21st century look. The combination of indigo upholstery on the chairs with the glass table and mirrored walls is eclectic, exciting and very blue.

Denim

Denim blue is now perceived as a color in its own right, but it is in fact a faded indigo. The reason denim fades as it does is because it is woven with a blue warp (the threads that show on the surface) and a white weft (the horizontal threads that make the underside light), so as the fabric wears, the white starts to show through.

[ABOVE] A stunning geometric chair with an op art fabric is set against a trellis painted in a soft denim blue. It makes a distinctly friendlier statement than black and white, which would perhaps have been a more obvious choice.

[OPPOSITE] A treasure chest, wittily accessorized with antlers and chains, makes a distinctly blue statement in a dark wood paneled hall.

nstead of artificial and plastic paint finishes, try a limewash or a chalky emulsion paint. You will get a great effect naturally created by the light and the paint itself. It dries with texture.

When testing limewash color, be sure to test in full sunlight, in the darkest part of the room, and somewhere in the middle as well. Limewash must be applied directly to bare surfaces: brick, cement, stone; you can strip surfaces with a wire brush. Plaster requires a newly skimmed surface. Limewashes can be sealed with acrylic diluted with water.

Remember, the downside with limewash and similar finishes is that they cannot be cleaned. They can be dusted and vacuumed but not washed. This may not be an ideal surface for a child's room, but then, how often in a lifetime does one wash one's walls? The beautiful effect is worth it.

Francesca
Wezel

Blue Jeans

Denim is a youthful, carefree color, forever associated with jeans. As a paint color, it makes a good backdrop for ethnic statuary or natural objects such as driftwood and seashells. But it can be sophisticated too. Plain denim fabric will brighten up a traditional interior and add an irreverent touch to a seriously modern monochrome scheme. The best neutral colors for denims are the textured limewashes with an almost imperceptible hint of cream or pink, to add a touch of warmth. All the bright pinks are great accent colors for denim.

Denim Technique:
THE RALPH LAUREN DENIM TECHNIQUE

For a bright denim:
RALPH LAUREN COWGIRL BLUE GLAZE OVER RALPH LAUREN BLUEPRINT

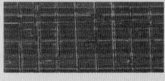

Darker denims:
RALPH LAUREN COWGIRL BLUE GLAZE OVER RALPH LAUREN DENIM HEATHER

RALPH LAUREN AGED NAVY GLAZE OVER RALPH LAUREN STUCCO WHITE

An amazing navy lacquer:
KELLY HOPPEN SHANGHAI BLUE.

The accents:
FRANCESCA'S PAINTS BENJAMIN'S OXBLOOD

FRANCESCA'S PAINTS LOUISE'S ORANGE

FRANCESCA'S PAINTS REBECCA'S RED

[ABOVE LEFT] A totally amazing tangle of metal shapes and off-cuts stuck to an exterior wall and painted blue. It's a strong and stylish statement that stands boldly out from the crowd.

[ABOVE RIGHT] Dark blue is an unusual choice of color for a fireplace, but it's reminiscent of slate, and that's why it works so well. It looks particularly brilliant here with the stacks of terracotta and ochre baskets on either side.

[OPPOSITE] In this case it's the art on the walls that sets the blue tone. The shimmering panels dominate the room and the rest of the décor is kept neutral.

Deep, dark blue is a sophisticated, modern color that feels like home. It answers the need for an intense hue that is easy to live with because it does not crowd in on the space like the yellows and reds. Blue is strong, yet it recedes, retaining an impression of larger volumes of space. From all that I've seen, I think it's the modern urban blue that provides the perfect solution for the cutting-edge interior as the pendulum swings away from space-enhancing, any-color-as-long-as-it's-white schemes.

If you ever needed proof that blue is the color of now, here it is. The stunning sculptural bench is the only color statement in the room, and it's so strong you can't take your eyes off it.

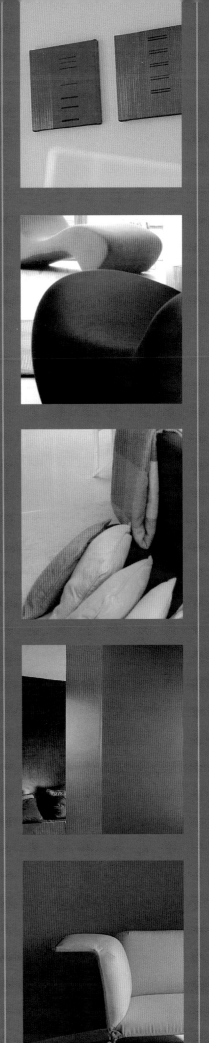

sharp-edged urban blues

Colorful Blues

To take a brilliantly true blue into a cutting edge scheme, it can be a case of more actually being less. If you use a palette of colors that are just as intense as each other but from opposite ends of the spectrum, you will achieve a pleasing balance. But pleasing balances are not for everyone—for the adventurous, blue can be license to play with daring combinations, including primary reds and yellows, deep vivid greens, and wicked touches of black. Anything goes with these sharp urban blues.

[OPPOSITE] In a double-height loft, a glass staircase skims past a colorful wall of strong modern blue. Accent colors are as bold as the architecture.

[ABOVE] Stunning blue shapes in a loft setting. The strong blue and red fabrics really make the most of the sculptural furniture. Again, it's the only color statement that's needed.

[LEFT] Simplicity itself as the fierce blue column offers vivid contrast to the brilliant red wall.

"There is blue in practically every room in my house.
I guess it is my favorite color. Of course it's a classic and
looks great with white (it's that all time favorite
combination), but I also love blue with pink and with orange.
All different shades of blue look pretty together as well.
You can really almost work with blue as a neutral."

MARY MULCAHY, LES INDIENNES

[OPPOSITE] Christmas decorations at the home of Paula Pryke, the famous London florist. Blue isn't a color traditionally associated with Christmas, but with the addition of silver and sparkle, it works a treat.

[ABOVE] The bedroom in Paula Pryke's London loft is separated from the living area by a sliding blue screen. The amazing check bed linen with its attendant cushions is a joyous addition.

[LEFT] Strong blue and tomato red at a work station in a loft apartment. The bold colors are cleverly restricted to one wall, and the steel portholes add that necessary touch of wit and sparkle.

Cool Blues

For a smart, witty look, use the urban blues with silver, with metallic sheers, lots of mirror glass, wooden floors, and animal prints. Add a beautiful glass vase and a white orchid for the last word in urban chic.

Some thoughts on urban blues:

Periwinkle is a fairly conventional color, but using it with an unusual shade of tobacco makes it very new again. Clear sky blue is a young, contemporary color—always use it with creams such as unbleached linen or taupe, but never white.

It's important to find the correct paint colors to use—weathered and slightly off shades are always best as they reflect the light so well and never look too new. Stick with the mellow colors, never electric or too bland.

Indigo and midnight blue, colors we haven't seen in a while, are becoming popular again. Peacock blue, or a really circa 18th-century Chinese blue, are great with acid green and make for a very 21st-century look. And I think silver is going to be really big with blue, it's very much a coming look for chic blue.

It's interesting to note that every fabric collection has more blues in it than any other color; weathered linen fabrics in pale shades of blue, washed and weathered matlasse, and rich blue paisleys. Ikat-like ethnic fabrics are great for upholstery, especially in blue, as there are five different blues mixed into the pattern.

Albert Sardelli, Brunschwig & Fils

[ABOVE] An amazing home with sea views. The dining area has blue upholstered chairs that are not only comfortable but extremely stylish. Blue is the color of choice, and it is reflected from the sea and the sky into the room thanks not only to the chairs but the blue-grey metallic hue of the ceiling panel.

[TOP RIGHT] Bold blue walls with accent colors used on the insides of the archways and on inset panels in the ceiling. This is a brilliant way to get color bouncing around a room. Accents here are soft ochres and delicious pinks.

[RIGHT] Shades of blue on a folding door, painted in diamond shapes. The diamonds on the wall opposite are perfect modern accent shades: strong green and tomato red.

"These are my favorite blues
in the paint range by
Benjamin Moore:
Ol' Blue Eyes 2064-30 and
Brilliant Blue 2065-30.
They are both very strong blues."

LIBBY CAMERON

Ol' Blue Eyes 2064-30

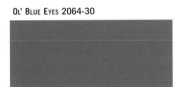

Brilliant Blue 2065-30

[OPPOSITE] Another shot of the stunning seaside home shown overleaf. In the seating area, a curved wall of brilliant blue outdoes the sea and sky. The pale blue upholstery of the loungers is a refreshing splash of cool.

[ABOVE] Artworks and decorative objects with presence can be your starting point for a modern blue scheme. These sculptural pieces from Majolica Works would be impossible to ignore. They have been photographed here against a stunning orange background.

PHOTOGRAPH BY JOEL CHESTER FILDES, COURTESY MAJOLICA WORKS

[LEFT] The big bang comes from the enigmatic blue artworks that dominate this room. Accent colors are orange and a tiny flash of pink.

It is time for a bit of unashamed luxury. Time to delight in violet-blue velvets and lilac-colored silks shot with silver to give them a glorious voluptuousness. Have you noticed how the same blue in cotton looks completely different in silk? Color practically vibrates off silk, and velvet colors feel dense and endless, as if you are drowning in them. Advances in dying technologies now mean we are spoiled for choice with rich and rare fabrics that will keep the intensity of color. These wonderful fabrics can be battened onto walls or thrown over a bed or endlessly reflected in mirrors, creating a look that calls for over-the-top touches such as gilding, columns, and pillars. Blue in all its manifestations is the perfect color range for luxury and for looking good: greens and yellows are unflattering to skin tones, reds too hot, and whites too risky.

The luxury of the Pharaohs evoked by Napoleonic gilded furniture. Against the colors of the dark and light wood, the almost obsessive use of navy gives this room a real feeling of opulence.

sensual blues

[LEFT] In this Belgravia home, dark navy and a luscious blue have been used to create the ultimate sensual dining room, a room devoted to pleasurable times. The tall blue vases are slim enough not to sever eye-contact and the gleam of glass and silver are set off magnificently by the dark background.

[BELOW] The smartest of kitchens has walls of blue lacquer and walls of mirror glass. Once again the lighting has been very well thought out and the sparkle of mirror and blue is the ultimate in luxurious surroundings.

[LEFT] Navy and silver are a surefire way of creating a sense of luxury. This wallpaper has a subtle silvery pattern, and the table lamps have been painted silver. It's luxury that does not shout out loud.

[BELOW] An opulent bathroom with subtle, flattering lighting, deep blue slate walls, plenty of glass, and sparkling chrome. It is totally modern without a trace of stark white.

Top of the Range Paints

For deep, dark, satisfying paint colors, you will need flat, or dead-flat oil-based paints, a limewash which dries to a velvety, matt finish, or good quality matt emulsions. You need paints with a high percentage of pigment to give them the satisfying depth that spells luxury. Accent paintwork with gold or silver to get that essential sensual gleam—it could be a gilded trim or a gilded mirror or picture frame. And while on the subject of picture frames, I think ornate empty gilded frames make wonderfully enigmatic statements. You get the joy of a beautiful frame without the problem of overwhelming a painting with an intense and striking color.

[ABOVE] All the luxury touches in one place. Glass and sparkle against a dark blue wall. The glass jar is filled with gleaming pearls and shells, and the Venetian mirror sparkles it all right back.

[LEFT] A wonderful floor design has been created in shades of blue, grey blue, and off white blue. Note how subtle yet stunning the colors are, forming a sensational dining room floor. It is of course advisable to use very good quality paints and add a top glaze to prevent wear and tear and too much fading.

[OPPOSITE] Here the deep pigment used in this London home adds a sense of luxury, comfort and elegance. One can imagine glamorous dinner parties with fine food and sparkling conversation.

"So many paints look flat. I like looking into a color that is saturated with pigment."

Tom Helme, Farrow & Ball

sensual blues

135

"Living in the South, where the heat can send one to bed,
introducing blue into an interior can help cool down the temperature.
I love a pale blue-green-grey in the entrance hall, paired with lovely
oriental rugs, polished mahogany furniture, gilded mirrors, a crystal
candelabra, a little ebony and a glass of bourbon!"

JACKYE LANHAM

[OPPOSITE] Blue and silver set off a beautiful Chinese armoire, a pair of Chinese chairs, and shapely pots. There is a lovely feeling of calm and balance about this room.

[ABOVE] Even on a modest scale, navy blue and silver still read as luxury. Here all it has taken is a blue fireplace, a bit of silver, and gold paint on the mirror and the chair, silver candlesticks and the gleam of a nautilus shell.

[RIGHT] The sensual tones used on accessories in this rather contemporary and very comfortable room gives a very 21st-century look.

Luxury Fabrics

[LEFT] Schumacher is making blue and cream striped tickings from silk and wonderful silk velvets that combine the blues with putty and cream.
© F. SCHUMACHER & CO.

[OPPOSITE] Ironic take on the traditional sitting room. The elaborate gilt mirrors reflect a room with a difference. Where you would expect chintz you have dramatic dark blue silk curtains with sweeping purple swags and sofas upholstered in a dark blue velour. The whole room, while deeply luxurious, is dramatically subverted.

Reds and blues are poles apart. Where they mingle the relationship can be anything from delightfully subtle to deeply unsettling. A successful combination produces some wonderful colors from the delicacy of a wisteria bloom to the incomparable richness of deep purple.

"The reason 'dirty' shades of paint color work so well is because they have natural pigments like burnt amber and raw umber, so the colors have a special vintage, unique look that goes with everything."

FRANCESCA WEZEL, FRANCESCA'S PAINTS

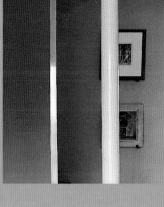

red blues

The fabulous creamy sheen of the eggs, the white coral, and the black bust echo the marble of the fireplace in this lovely room with pale "dirty" mauve walls.

Lavender and Hydrangea

These delicate hues demand attention. They are quite difficult to use as all-over neutrals, but when done right, they can look amazing. These colors come on the pale side of the red-blue axis. When it veers towards red it starts out as lavender and then wanders off into the dusky pinks. Going the other way, and adding more blue, you get that delicate but positive color of hydrangeas in full bloom.

[ABOVE] This is a very bright, actually quite difficult color, but it works well with the lime green behind it. Lime green works well with many shades of blue.

[LEFT] An alcove in a summer home where a "clean" shade of mauve has been used, which works brilliantly in bright sunlight.

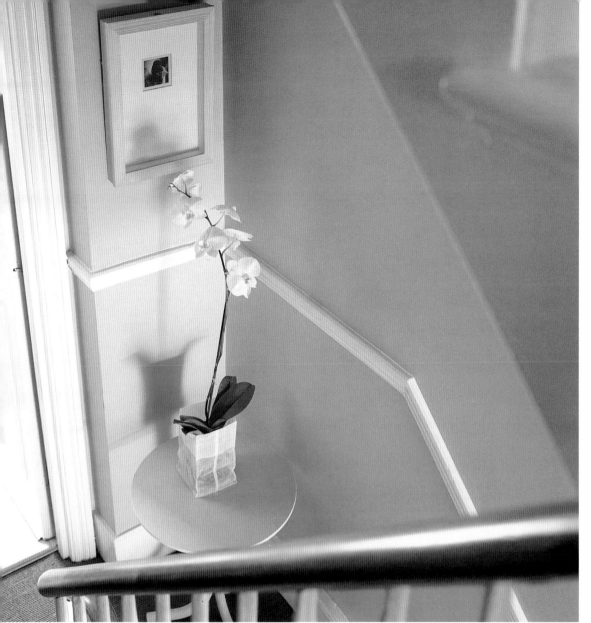

[LEFT] A brilliant example of how sunlight affects blue. In this hallway, a lavender changes to mauve on a sloping section of wall.

[LEFT] This is a good mauve. The cupboard doors are a "dirty" color that goes well with white, wood, and stainless steel and ends up looking modern.

"In a blue room I can't resist a flash of pink."

SASHA WADDELL

Lavender can look stunning in period houses. It's a totally unexpected color, but it goes remarkably well with dark polished wood, white paintwork and pretty printed fabrics. I've always thought that hydrangea looks great in the country and beside the seaside as a rubbed-back, weathered paint finish on wooden doors and shutters, because it is a color that responds well to sunlight, weak or strong.

Mixing and Matching

In a modern setting these colors work well as big blocks of color, such as a feature wall or a run of cupboard doors. I think they look great with strong true blues, deep purples, reds and pinks, and positively stunning with silver and glass. A good neutral would be a pink-tinged white or a slubby linen color. As a rule, pale red blues are not quite so happy with greens and yellows which rather diminish their subtlety.

"Tone-on-tone walls are non-invasive, stylish, and provide a serene background. Warm your tone-on-tone room up with small touches of color in fabrics, accessories, and flowers."

FRANCESCA WEZEL,
FRANCESCA'S PAINTS

[OPPOSITE TOP] Caribbean bonanza of color that breaks every rule in the book. Again a good example of how well these colors work in bright sunlight.

[OPPOSITE BOTTOM] An unusual shade for a stair carpet gives a white painted hall a real lift.

[RIGHT] Various shades of lavender working well together, using the lightest shade on the ceiling and the darkest on the bed cover. A row of black-and-white photos on the wall above the bed are the perfect understated touch.

[BELOW] Flooded with Provençal sunlight, lavender looks at its best accented with white and a bunch of the real thing.

[OPPOSITE TOP] This soft and mellow aubergine color is an unexpectedly brilliant idea in that it makes the angles of this attic bedroom an asset rather than a disadvantage. I love the quilt echoing the same soft period color.

[OPPOSITE BOTTOM] A soothing bedroom with a distinctly masculine flavor thanks to a measured choice of mauves and browns and an unusual Chinese bed. Bedrooms should never be too startling.

[LEFT] You think of lavender as a pale, polite color that goes with old lace, but when you see it growing in the garden of this French home, you can see how intense the color can be.

[ABOVE] An almost aubergine mauve has been used here on the wall, which is painted to look like stone. The mirror with its brilliant slashes of blue works really well. It's an unusual color combination, but it is subtle and it works.

[RIGHT AND BELOW] A bit of Napoleonic grandeur here in an Empire room, boldly decorated with a hand-blocked wallpaper in a stunning shade of violet with gilded detail. The room deserves its chandelier, and the red drapes look stunning. The lampshades are very smartly dark blue with red trim. The whole room feels elegantly different.

Violet

This color, absolutely slap-bang between red and blue, is full of contradictions. On the one hand, it has amazing energy, resonating as it does on a very short wavelength and then tipping over into ultraviolet, which resonates so fast it is actually invisible to the human eye. On the other hand, violet is supposed to induce feelings of introspection—so either way it's quite a tricky color to use decoratively.

Not a Shrinking Violet

The new violets are an enigmatic not-quite purple and not-quite blue range of colors that in the hands of a real professional look perfect and modern. It makes for an idiosyncratic look that is great at night with

clever lighting, but perhaps not such a good choice for a room streaming with sunlight, only because violet tends to absorb light.

I would use it as an accent color, as cushion covers or throws, maybe a painted alcove displaying glass or silver on glass shelves, so you would get a play between dark and light, between shimmer and enigma. It would be a great accent color in a soft blue room, really giving it some depth. I wouldn't use a brilliant white anywhere near violet—it's just too harsh, a creamy white or a pinky white would be perfect. Pale silver greys would look good, too, but I'd avoid the apricot- to yellow-based neutrals altogether. If you want to add a little fleck of something shocking—I'd go for shocking pink.

[ABOVE] A mural panel has a background of pale mauve—almost an azure blue—that shows off the massed floral composition. A laid back yellow wall adds a sunshine touch picked up by the upholstery on the side chairs.

[LEFT] Pale blue walls and faded rose chintz are a wonderful combination, like the colors of an antique Aubusson carpet. The room is much enhanced by the blue and mauve painted doors, so much more appealing that the traditional white gloss route.

[RIGHT] Strong colors in the family room; a strong violet blue on the walls with lovely color accents. The idea of using a contrasting color in the revel of an arch is great—orange in this case—and if you use a gloss paint it makes for wonderful reflections of light.

[OPPOSITE TOP] A wall of cupboards that is anything but bland. Mauve is accented here with greens, oranges and yellows and outlined with white. It's a work of art in itself.

[BOTTOM BOTTOM] A stunning courtyard—a very glamorous use of a murky shade of violet. It is smart and urban and a wonderful way to treat a tiny outside space.

PAINT COLORS

In Francesca's Paints Fresh Collection there are three wonderful shades that could be used in almost any scheme in the Lavender, Mauve, Lilac, Violet range. They are ideal for walls, for ceilings, and for woodwork, either used together or separately, as they are three strengths of the same soft, elegant, slightly off-kilter shade:

FRANCESCA'S PAINTS LAVENDER 1

FRANCESCA'S PAINTS LAVENDER 11

FRANCESCA'S PAINTS LAVENDER 111

A slightly deeper yet equally subtle shade (and subtle is needed with these mauvy colors):
BENJAMIN MOORE'S SPRING LILAC 1388

Other good shades for walls:
BENJAMIN MOORE SUGAR PLUM 1394

BENJAMIN MOORE MISTY LILAC 2071-70

Good background colors for these mauvy shades:
RALPH LAUREN PETTICOAT WHITE

BENJAMIN MOORE OYSTER 2115-70

"Don't be afraid of color, you will love what it does to your life."

Francesca Wezel, Francesca's Paints

Purple

Purple dyes were never easy to manufacture, but once chemists got the hang of it in the mid-19th century, the color just erupted. The fashion-conscious French went wild for it, and the silk-dyers of Lyons put it into production, naming it mauve after the delicate purple of the mallow flower. Call it mauve, call it eggplant or aubergine, it's a wonderfully regal color that adds drama to both traditional and modern interiors. Deep, deep purple is the perfect red-blue compromise. It's neither hot nor cold, neither masculine nor feminine, but it is sumptuous and decadent, moody and evocative, rich and jewel-like.

Stephen Falcke of Johannesburg has designed homes, hotels, lodges, seaside retreats, ships, and board rooms all over the world. He won the prestigious Andrew Martin Designer of the year award for the Saxon Hotel—possibly one of the most beautiful hotels in the world.

Falcke—who never seems to be anywhere for more than two days, yet always has time for his clients and his friends—loves the color purple. When I spoke to him in Johannesburg, he gave me his thoughts on using this amazing shade belonging to the blue family. Stephanie Hoppen

Purple is papal—it is also the color of royalty and as such it demands attention—particularly in its purest and deepest tones. It needs a fearless quality and a lot of passion to use it in an all-over way, but when used well it is magnificent, poetic, dramatic, and jewel like. It is also a powerful, passionate accent color and can be used with many background shades of grey, lavender, and taupe. In its paler hues it is the color of the Jacaranda trees I grew up with in South Africa, of lavender, and of the palest shade of bougainvillea. These softer shades, too, require great attention to get the correct shade so that the effect is not too candy-like. What can be really interesting is the use of many of the deep and less intense shades of purple used together as they work layer upon layer extremely seductively and with a sense of enormous luxury. Most of all, I simply love purple.

Stephen Falcke

"It's a truism that deep colors can make a room seem smaller, but rich tones also create a moody, rustic feel which works well in areas that need to feel warm and welcoming. It's not by chance that restaurants are often decorated in dark colors with lighting that's soft and subdued to create the right ambience."

STEPHANIE HOPPEN

[OPPOSITE] A very chic bedroom with a luxurious 30s Savoy feeling. The rich, deep purple bed is set against a pale lavender wall, a fortuitous marriage of the top and bottom ends of the range of purple hues balanced with a beautiful brass pot.

[ABOVE] A stunning purple accent: bottles of amethyst glass and mauve orchids. It is a color statement that cannot be ignored.

[RIGHT] An imaginative accent in a rich purple room, this blue-black console table reflects back the purple, and the spiky aloe plants lift the room into the 21st century.

[LEFT] A fireplace wall in a neutral bedroom is painted a stunning shade of deep purple. The black fireplace almost disappears into it.

[BELOW] A principally donkey brown room where various shades of purple and aubergine are used in the accessories rather than on the walls.

[OPPOSITE] Another stunning example of the use of dark and pale shades of reddish colored blues. The deep purple walls, which could be oppressive, are leavened with a classical mural painted onto a lavender-blue panel.

All or Nothing

Rich purple works either as an accent color—a cashmere throw on an all-white sofa—or as a bold backdrop of walls and ceiling. It goes brilliantly with all the pale red-blues—the pale violets and lavenders—but because purple is so overwhelming, dark blues like deep indigo would tend to get ignored in its presence.

For darker shades to be used for woodwork, doors and, possibly, excitement, how about:

BENJAMIN MOORE HYDRANGEA 1390

RALPH LAUREN PURPLE DAHLIA.

BENJAMIN MOORE FIRE AND ICE 1392

I think that the different shades of lavender, mauve, and lilac go best of all when one layers them from palest to darkest in the same tone, but all the shades of bright pink and fuschia work wonderfully as accent colors with them all, as does a hint of the ever popular lime green—the favorite accent color of this new century. These colors are best used as flowers, objects, a cushion or a small chair rather than as a paint color, unless of course you are looking for the "rock chic" effect.

Dark colors usually make a room look smaller but they can also create a warm and moody atmosphere. When you use warm dark colors like mulberry or eggplant in a room with much paler walls, a truly dramatic, yet also warm and mellow, effect can be obtained.

The Neutrals and Complementaries

Soft whites set off eggplant colors wonderfully. Olive greens are the natural complementary color, while bright pea greens and limes look cutting edge with the brighter shades of purple. If you are going for flourish, regal purple has a natural affinity with gold—think grand gilt frames and wall sconces and damn the consequences.

[OPPOSITE TOP] Using purple as the accent color in a room that is basically neutral with ethnic touches. Purple and cream are used together in an imaginative way.

[OPPOSITE BOTTOM] An unusual 30s cabinet flanked with purple curtains. The rosy pink panels on the cabinet make for an unusual color combination.

[ABOVE] The interesting striped curtaining pulls together all the elements in this room. It has wonderful purple walls, dark blue lampshades, gilded frames, and lime green upholstery.

[RIGHT] A little detail of a bookshelf that shows how accents can make a room zing. Here a row of purple-bound books are jauntily counterpointed with bright red rose hips and touches of orange.

Blue is a color that lends itself to the individual style. It's got everything to offer from deep dark riches to wisps of cloudy skies via colors that are almost green and almost pink. The eclectic decorator will revel in the possibilities, juxtaposing old and new, mixing textures and styles, indulging in murals, trompe-l'oeil, and other witticisms with careless abandon. But there's a fine line between delightfully eclectic and a room that's an unnerving, unsettling mess—and in my experience the line is usually color. If the colors speak to each other, then textures and styles can jumble about as much as they want to. And that's because color affects people—it elicits emotions—and blue, which is predominant in these gloriously individual homes, soothes and calms like no other color can.

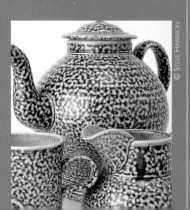

eclectic blue

Ethnic Blue

The blues of North Africa and southern Spain range from the ice-blue limewash typical of the cool houses of Chechaouen, a sacred village perched high in the Rif mountains, to intense ultramarine blues and the searingly blue glazes found on tiles and brickwork. In these hot climates, blue brings both a soothing, calming respite from heat, as well as strong and vibrant blocks of color that refuse to be bleached out by the noonday sun.

The Ethnic Mix

Team up the ethnic blues with dazzling greens and reds, sunshine yellows and exuberant patterns. Don't treat them too seriously, these blues can take just about anything from colorful mosaics to bright enamels and the glow of colored glass. For the neutral shade, pick a paler shade of blue or a soft limestone white.

To Get the Look

De La Cuona Ltd

De La Cuona Ltd

You don't have to re-decorate to "blueify"—you can get the effect with flowers and accessories that you probably already own. You could add a mass of blue flowers ranging from gorgeous displays of tall delphiniums and great buckets of hydrangeas to shy little pansies or anemones in bowls. As far as accessories go, blue glass makes a robust contribution and it doesn't have to be expensive—they make wonderful blue glass in Mexico now. And as for ceramics, explore the wonderful new Majolica ceramics and imported porcelains, which are available as expensive designer one-offs as well as cheerful, mass-produced items. The idea is to catch the eye as you enter a room—faced with a stunning blue accent makeover, no one will notice you haven't redecorated.

De La Cuona Ltd

De La Cuona Ltd

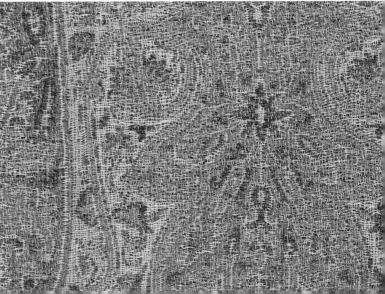

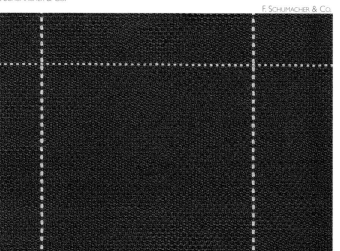

to get the look

"The best way to capture the true intensity of blue flowers is to use one type en masse. This is illustrated perfectly in the English countryside in early May when bluebells shimmer in beech woods and magically reflect the sky. Arranging soft, abundant clouds of blue hydrangea captures this glory, as do spires of lapis delphinium. There are so many beautiful blue flowers to use in one's interior, the joy is yours to behold, be it a single perfect anemone in a Delft egg cup or a mass of cobalt agapanthus in an oversized glass vase."

ROBBIE HONEY

"Other flowers that work with blue blooms: white peonies look fabulous in a blue room mixed with blue blooms. Bluebells are beautiful when presented alone in blue-and-white jugs, and forget-me-nots look soft and delicate when mixed with the sensuous lily-of-the-valley. Another perfect presentation is a blue hydrangea in a pale yellow room. But, ultimately, you can't beat white blooms to complement the soft British blues!"

JOHN CARTER,
CELEBRATED LONDON FLORIST

Blue Flowers:

VIRGINIA BLUEBELLS (MERTENSIA VIRGINICA)
COMMON VIOLET (VIOLA PAPILIONACEA)
WILD VIOLET (VIOLACEAE)
TALL BLUE LETTUCE (LACTUCA VILLOSA)
SELF-HEAL (PRUNELLA VULGARIS)
VENUS'S LOOKING-GLASS (TRIODANIS PERFOLIATA)
TALL BELLFLOWER (CAMPANULA AMERICANA)
CREEPING BELLFLOWER (CAMPANULA RAPUNCULOIDES)
HAREBELL (CAMPANULA ROTUNDIFOLIA)
SMOOTH RUELLIA (RUELLIA STREPENS)
BLUETS (HOUSTONIA CAERULEA)
WATER SPEEDWELL (VERONICA ANAGALLIS-AQUATICA)
GERMANDER SPEEDWELL (VERONICA CHAMAEDRYS)
FORGET-ME-NOT, (MYOSOTIS SCORPIOIDES)
FLAX (LINUM USITATISSIMUM)
MOSS PHLOX (PHLOX SUBULATA)
PERIWINKLE (VINCA MINOR)
BLUE-EYED GRASS (SISYRINCHIUM)
ROUND-LOBED / SHARP-LOBED HEPATICA
   (HEPATICA AMERICANA / ACUTILOBA)
CHICORY (CICHORIUM INTYBUS)
NEW ENGLAND ASTER (ASTER NOVAE-ANGLIAE)
BERGAMOT (MONARDA FISTULOSA)
BLUE FLAG IRIS (IRIS PRISMATICA)
VIPER'S BUGLOSS/BLUEWEED (ECHIUM VULGARE)
PICKEREL WEED (PONTEDERIA CORDATA)
CLOSED GENTIAN (GENTIANA ANDREWSII)
NIGHTSHADE (SOLANUM DULCAMARA)
ALFALFA (MEDICAGO SATIVA)
COW VETCH (VICIA CRACCA)
BUGLE (AJUGA REPTANS)
COMMON/MARSH SKULLCAP (SCUTELLARIA EPILOBIIFOLIA)
PALE SPIKE LOBELIA (LOBELIA SPICATA)
SQUARE-STEMMED MONKEY FLOWER (MIMULUS RINGENS)
BLUE VERVAIN (VERBENA HASTATA)
BLAZING STAR (LIATRIS SPICATA)
LUPINS (LUPINUS POLYPHYLLUS)
MORNING GLORY (POMOEA PURPUREA)
HYDRANGEA (HYDRANGEA MACROPHYLLA)

"Each piece of this exquisite blue glass from master artist Anthony Stern is blown by hand; no two pieces are exactly the same. They are created only once a year, when the glass furnaces are scrubbed, because the intense, saturated, cobalt-blue color can only be achieved in an absolutely clean furnace."

Stephanie Hoppen

"Steve Harrison finds his inspiration in the past. His one-off pieces, design commissions for museums and private collections, reinvent an 18th-century aesthetic, and will be treasured antiques of the future."

Stephanie Hoppen

"Classic blue and white is given a most 21st-century interpretation by the designers at Majolica Works; fresh, modern and wholly original."

STEPHANIE HOPPEN

resources

PAINT COMPANIES

ANNIE SLOAN; Oxford, UK
P: 01865.768666
www.anniesloan.com

BEHR; Santa Ana, CA, USA
P: 800.854.0133
www.behr.com

BENJAMIN MOORE; Montvale,
NJ, USA
P: 800.344.0400
www.benjaminmoore.com

COLE & SON; London, UK
P: 020.7376.4628
www.cole-and-son.com

COLOR WHEEL PAINTS; Orlando,
FL, USA
P: 800.749.6810
www.colorwheelpaint.com

CRAIG & ROSE; Fife, Scotland,
UK
P: 01383.740000
www.craigandrose.com

CROWN PAINTS; Lancashire, UK
P: 01254.704951
www.crownpaint.co.uk

DULUX; Slough, UK
P: 01753.550555
www.dulux.co.uk

EARTHBORN PAINTS; Cheshire, UK
P: 01928.734171
www.earthbornpaints.co.uk

ECOS ORGANIC PAINTS; Lancs, UK
P: 01524.852371
www.ecospaints.com

FARROW & BALL; Dorset, UK
P: 01202.876141
www.farrow-ball.com

FIRED EARTH INTERIORS;
Oxfordshire, UK
P: 01295.812088
www.firedearth.com

FRANCESCA WEZEL, Francesca's
Paints, London, UK
P: 020.7228 7694
www.francescaspaint.com

GEORGINA BARROW NATURAL PAINTS;
Gloucestershire, UK
P: 01451.861040
www.naturalpaints.org.uk

HAMMERITE; Slough, UK
P: 01661.830000
www.hammerite.com

HERITAGE PAINTS; Slough, UK
P: 01753.550555
www.heritagepaints.co.uk

KELLY HOPPEN INTERIORS, Paints
www.kellyhoppen.com

KELLY-MOORE PAINT; San Carlos,
CA, USA
P: 650.592.8337
www.kellymoore.com

LAURA ASHLEY; Fort Hill, SC,
USA
P: 803.396.7744
www.lauraashley-usa.com

LEYLAND; West Yorkshire, UK
P: 01924.354000
www.leyland-paints.co.uk

MARSTON & LANGINGER; London,
UK
P: 020.7881.5783
www.marston-and-
langinger.com

MARTHA STEWART SIGNATURE; USA
P: 888.562.7842
www.marthastewart.com

NUTSHELL NATURAL PAINTS; South
Brent, UK
P: 01364.73801
www.nutshellpaints.com

PAINT & PAPER LIBRARY;
London, UK
P: 020.7823.7755
www.paintlibrary.co.uk

PAINTWORKS; London, UK
P: 020.7720.8018
www.paintworks.co.uk

PRATT & LAMBERT PAINTS; Buffalo,
NY, USA
P: 800.289.7728
www.prattandlambert.com

RALPH LAUREN PAINT; NY, USA
P: 800.379.7656
rlhome.polo.com

RESTORATION HARDWARE; Corte
Madera, CA, USA
P: 800.762-1005
www.restorationhardware.com

SHERWIN-WILLIAMS; USA
P: 800.832.2541
www.sherwin-williams.com

SURFACE FX, INC.; Santa Barbara,
CA, USA
P: 805.963.3126
www.surfacefxinc.com

SYDNEY HARBOUR PAINT COMPANY;
Los Angeles, CA, USA
P: 213.228.8440
www.sydneyharbourpaints.com

ZOFFANY; Hertfordshire, UK
P: 0870.830.0350
www.zoffany.com

FABRIC HOUSES

ADO INTERNATIONAL; Spartanburg,
SC, USA
P: 800.845.0918
www.ado-usa.com

BAILEY & GRIFFIN; New York,
NY, USA
P: 212.832.4160

BEACON HILL; Mansfield, MA,
USA
P: 800.333.3776
www.beaconhilldesign.com

BENNETT SILKS; Stockport, UK
P: 0161.476.8600
www.bennett-silks.co.uk

BERGAMO FABRICS; New York,
NY, USA
P: 212.888.3333
www.bergamofabrics.com

BERY DESIGNS; London, UK
P: 020.7351.5797
www.berydesigns.com

BOUSSAC FADINI; Paris, France
P: 866.268.7722
www.boussac-fadini.fr

BRUNO TRIPLET; London, UK
P: 020.7823.9990
www.brunotriplet.co.uk

BRUNSCHWIG & FILS; North White
Plains, NY, USA
P: 416.968.0699
www.brunschwig.com

CABBAGES & ROSES; Bath, UK
P: 01225.859151
www.cabbagesandroses.com

CARLETON V; New York,
NY, USA
P: 212.355.4525

CHASE ERWIN SILKS; London, UK
P: 0208.875.1222
www.chase-erwin.com

CHELSEA TEXTILES; London, UK
P: 020.7584.0111
www.chelseatextiles.com

CHRISTOPHER HYLAND;
New York, NY, USA
P: 212.688.6121
www.christopherhyland.net

CHRISTOPHER NORMAN;
New York, NY, USA
P: 212.647.0303
www.christophernorman.com

CLARENCE HOUSE; New York,
NY, USA
P: 800.221.4704
www.clarencehouse.com

CLASSIC CLOTH; Plainville, KS,
USA
P: 785.434.2777
www.dessinfournir.com

CORAGGIO TEXTILES; New York,
NY, USA
P: 212.758.9885
www.coraggio.com

COWTAN & TOUT; West
Hollywood, CA, USA
P: 310.659.1423

DE LE CUONA LTD.; London, UK
P: 01753.830301
www.delecuona.com

DECORATORS WALK; New York, NY,
USA
P: 212.415.3955
www.decoratorswalk.com

DEDAR; Varese, Italy
P: 800.493.2209
www.dedar.com

DESIGNERS GUILD; London, UK
P: 020.7351.5775
www.designersguild.com

DIAMOND FOAM & FABRIC;
Los Angeles, CA, USA
P: 323.931.8148
www.diamondfoamandfabric.com

DONGHIA; London, UK
P: 800.366.4442
www.donghia.com

DURALEE FABRICS; Bay Shore,
NY, USA
P: 800.275.3872
www.duralee.cisnow.com

F. SCHUMACHER & CO.
P: 800.332.3384
www.fschumacher.com

FIRED EARTH INTERIORS
P: 01295.812088
www.firedearth.com

FORTUNY FABRIC; New York,
NY, USA
P: 212.753.7153
www.fortuny.com

GAINSBOROUGH SILK WEAVING CO.;
Suffolk, UK
P: 01787.372081
www.gainsborough.co.uk

GASTON Y DANIELA
P: 91.485.2590
www.gastonydaniela.com

GOLDING FABRICS; Archdale,
NC, USA
P: 336.883.9171
www.goldingfabrics.com

GRACIOUS HOME; New York,
NY, USA
P: 212.231.7800
www.gracioushome.com

GREENTEX UPHOLSTERY SUPPLIES, INC.;
New York, NY, USA
P: 800.762.8303
www.greentexinc.com

HENRY CALVIN FABRICS
P: 888.732.1996
www.henrycalvin.com

HINSON & CO.; New York,
NY, USA
P: 212.688.5538

HODSOLL MCKENZIE; London, UK
P: 020.7730.2877
www.hodsoll-mckenzie.com

HOLLY HUNT; New York, NY, USA
P: 212.755.6555
www.hollyhunt.com

IAN MANKIN; London, UK
P: 020.7722.0997

IKEA
P: 0845.355.1141
www.ikea.co.uk

JAGTAR; London, UK
P: 020.7351.4220
www.jagtar.co.th

JIM THOMPSON
P: 800.262.0336
www.jimthompson.com

JOHN HUTTON TEXTILES
P: 888.787.7827
www.johnhuttontextiles.com

JOHN ROBSHAW
P: 800.231.0038
www.johnrobshaw.com

KATHRYN IRELAND FABRICS
P: 310.315.4351
www.kathrynirelandfabrics.com

KRAVET, INC.
P: 516.293.2000
www.kravet.com

KREISS
P: 800.574.3771
www.kreiss.com

LAURA ASHLEY
P: 0871.230.2301
www.lauraashley.com

LEE JOFA
P: 800.453.3563
www.leejofa.com

MARY MULCAHY, Les Indiennes,
Tuscon, Arizona, USA
P:520.881 8122
www.mulcahydesign.com

MALABAR; London, UK
P: 020.7501.4200
www.malabar.co.uk

MANUEL CANOVAS
P: 020.8877.6440

MICHAEL LEVINE FABRIC
P: 213.622.6259

MIKHAIL PIETRANEK, Royal
Deeside; Scotland, UK
P: 01339.887744
www.scottish-textiles.co.uk

THE NATURAL FABRIC COMPANY;
Oxfordshire, UK
P: 01295.730064
www.naturalfabriccompany.com

NAUTICA; New York, NY, USA
P: 212.541.5757
www.nautica.com

NOBILIS FONTAN; London, UK
P: 020.7351.7878
www.nobilis.fr

NORDIC STYLE; London, UK
P: 020.7351.1755
www.nordicstyle.com

OLD WORLD WEAVERS;
New York, NY, USA
P: 212.355.7186
www.old-world-weavers.com

OSBORNE & LITTLE; London, UK
P: 020.7352.1456
www.osborneandlittle.com

PAPER MOON; London, UK
P: 020.7624.1198
www.papermoon.co.uk

PAYNE FABRICS; Grand Prairie,
TX, USA
P: 800.527.2517
www.paynefabrics.com

PERCHERON; London, UK
P: 020.7376.5992

PETER FASANO
P: 413.528.6872
www.peterfasano.com

PETER JONES; London, UK
P: 020.7730.3434
www.peterjones.co.uk

PIERRE FREY; New York,
NY, USA
P: 212.213.3099
www.pierrefrey.com

PINDLER & PINDLER, Inc.
P: 800.669.6002
www.pindler.com

POLLACK & ASSOCIATES;
New York, NY, USA
P: 212.627.7766
www.pollackassociates.com

R. JONES & ASSOCIATES
P: 214.951.0091
www.rjones.com

RALPH LAUREN CLASSIC FABRICS
AND WALLCOVERINGS
P: 888.475.7674
www.rlhome.polo.com

RAMM, SON & CROCKER; High
Wycombe, UK
P: 01494.603555
www.obelisk-interiors.co.uk

RAOUL TEXTILES
P: 805.965.1694
www.raoultextiles.com

RELIABLE FABRICS, INC.
P: 800.682.4567
www.reliablefabrics.com

ROBERT ALLEN
P: 800.333.3777
www.robertallendesign.com

ROGERS & GOFFIGON; New York, NY, USA
P: 212.888.3242

SAMUEL & SONS PASSEMENTERIE; New York, NY, USA
P: 212.704.8000

SANDERSON FABRIC
P: 01895.830044
www.sanderson-uk.com

SCALAMANDRÉ; Ronkonkoma, NY, USA
P: 631.467.8800
www.scalamandre.com

SDH
P: 707.864.8075
www.sdhonline.com

THE SILK TRADING CO.
P: 888.745.5302
www.silktrading.com

SILVER STATE
P: 801.972.6770

STEVEN FABRICS; Minneapolis, MN, USA
P: 800.328.2558
www.stevenfabrics.com

TITLEY & MARR; London, UK
P: 020.7351.2913

TRAVERS & CO.; New York, NY, USA
P: 212.888.7900
www.traversinc.com

WESTGATE FABRICS, INC.; Grand Prairie, TX, USA
P: 800.527.2517
www.westgatefabrics.com

WINHALL COLLECTION
P: 678.679.0011
www.winhallcollection.com

ZIMMER + ROHDE
P: 212.758.5357
www.zimmer-rohde.com

ZOFFANY
P: 0870.830.0350
www.zoffany.com

INTERIOR DESIGNERS

ALESSANDRA BRANCA; Chicago, IL, USA
P: 312.787.6123

DAVID KLEINBERG DESIGN ASSOC.; New York, NY, USA
P: 212.754.9500
E: dk@dkda.com
www.dkda.com

GINNY MAGHER, Atlanta, Georgia, USA
P: 404.231 1363
E: GmagherInt@aol.com

JACQUELYNNE P. LANHAM DESIGNS; Atlanta, GA, USA
P: 404.364.0472

JAMIE DRAKE; New York, NY, USA
P: 212.754.3099

JASON BELL; New York, NY, USA
P: 212. 339 0006
E: jbell@jbellinc.com

JEAN LARETTE
Larette Design
P: 415.464.0664
www.larettedesign.com

JOHN OETGEN; Atlanta, GA, USA
Oetgen Design, Inc.
P: 404.352.1112

JOSE SOLIS BETANCOURT
P: 202.659.8734

KELLY HOPPEN INTERIORS; London, UK
P:020.7471 3350
www.kellyhoppen.com

LARS BOLANDER; New York, NY, USA
P: 212.924.1000
E: chris@larsbolander.com
www.larsbolander.com

LIBBY CAMERON
LIBBY CAMERON LLC; New York, NY USA
P:914. 833 1414
www.libbycameron.com

MAIRA KOUTSOUDAKIS, Johannesburg, South Africa
P: 11.783 5965
E: maira@life.za.org

MARY DRYSDALE
Drysdale. Inc.
P: 202.588.0700

NANCY BRAITHWAITE INTERIORS; Atlanta, GA, USA
P: 404.355.1740

NINA CAMPBELL; London, UK
P: 020.7471 4270
www.ninacampbell.co.uk

SASHA WADDELL; London, UK
P: 020.7736 0766
E: info@sashawaddell.com
www.sashawaddell.com

SILVIO RECH AND LESLEY CARSTENS ARCHITECTURE & INTERIOR ARCHITECTURER; Johannesburg, South Africa
P: 11. 486 1525
E: aventarch@mweb.co.zalf

STEPHANIE STOKES; New York, NY, USA
P: 212.756 9922
E: stephanie@stephaniestokesinc.com

STEPHEN FALCKE; Johannesburg, South Africa
P: 11. 327 6730

T. KELLER DONOVAN, INC.; New York, NY, USA
P: 212.760.0537

JAMIE DRAKE; New York, NY, USA
P: 212.754.3099

TIM HOBBY, SPACE; Atlanta, GA, USA
P: 404.228 4600
www.spacemodern.com

VICENTE WOLF; New York, NY, USA
P: 212.465.0590
E: vincentewolf@verizon.net

CERAMICS AND GLASS

ANTHONY STERN
ANTHONY STERN GLASS; London, UK
P: 020. 7622 9463
www.anthonysternglass.com

STEVE HARRISON
P: 020.8482.4169
www.steveharrison.co.uk
enquiries@steveharrison.co.uk

WENDY JONES
MAJOLICA WORKS; Manchester, UK
P: 0161.835.3343

FLOWERS

JOHN CARTER FLOWERS; London, UK
P: 020.7731.5146

ROB HONEY; London, UK
P: 020.7720.3830

GENERAL

HOME DEPOT, USA
P: 800.553.3199
www.homedepot.com

HOME EXPO, USA
P: 757.412.1299
www.homeexpo.com

LOWE'S, USA
P: 800.445.6937
www.lowes.com

index

ACKNOWLEDGMENTS

There are so many wonderful friends and colleagues that have helped me, as they always do, to pull *Choosing Blue* together, and I feel I have to mention each and every one of them. This was indeed a shared experience and I know that without their enthusiasm and assistance my task would have been a very arduous one.

Jean Larette—a new friend, who brought the West Coast to London with her fresh approach to life and instant attention to our every request. Nina Campbell—who has been part of every book I have ever written, and I hope will always be so. Stephen Falcke of Johannesburg—a truly inspired designer and generous friend, and his assistant Marc Venter who helped get all the details together for us. Jackye Lanham—another inspired colleague who has become a very dear friend, and who also has never said no—yet! Tim Hobby of Space in Atlanta and his colleague Jennifer Brady—Atlanta would not be Atlanta without you both. Maria Koutsoudakis of Johannesburg for her inspiring color sense, and Silvio Rech and Lesley Carstens, architects extraordinaire. Libby Cameron who gave us acres of good decorating ideas with blues. Ginny Magher whose houses are always inspiring. Jason Bell—having found this rare talent at a Kipp's Bay showhouse, I have never let him be at peace to this day—and he never complains. Lars Bolander—a truly great designer always generous with assistance. Sasha Wadell for all her Gustavian style and Stephanie Stokes for her help to us at all times. All of you great designers have been wonderful to work with.

The fabric designers, too, have been of enormous assistance and have given many hours of their time to me discussing new trends, colors, and ways of using fabric. I have to mention, especially, Bernie de la Cuona, Mona Perlhagen of Chelsea Textiles, Albert Sardelli of Brunschwig & Fils, Susan North from F. Schumacher & Co., and Mary Mulcahy of Les Indiennes—all of them great taste makers.

Thank you also to Wendy Jones of Majolica Works, and Steve Harrison Ceramics for their help on the new styles in ceramics, and Anthony Stern for his exquisite blue glass. Georges Sheridan very kindly let us reproduce his stunning painting.

Rob Honey and John Carter helped me with blue flowers; Dorianne Weil spoke of living in blues; Tom Helme wrote of paint colors. Special thanks must go to Francesca Wezel who has taught me more about paint and color than I ever thought it was possible to know. Her kindness, patience, and joyous collaboration is something I treasure.

On the practical side of book making, it has been an enormous pleasure working with the inspiring Victoria Craven—a colleague and friend of a very special calibre. Martha Moran has been an extraordinary editor, making nothing of the Atlantic between us; Alexandra Maldonado for her beautiful book design; Cindy Richards for permissions given, and the wonderful Elisa Merlot at Andreas Von Einsiedel's archive for whom nothing was too much trouble.

Rubymaya Jaeck-Woodgate, my assistant, was thrown into *Choosing Blue* at the deep end and not only came up for air but has helped to get all the pieces together, especially in my many absences, with energy, willingness, intelligence, and a great sense of both fun and order.

Thank you one and all.

Stephanie
Hoppen